6·40

D1351948

Access to History
General Editor: Keith Randell

Reconstruction
and the Results of the
American Civil War
1865-1877

Alan Farmer

Hodder & Stoughton

A MEMBER OF THE HODDER HEADLINE GROUP

49489

The cover illustration is a portrait of Andrew Johnson by William Cooper (Courtesy of Topham Picture Point)

British Library Cataloguing in Publication Data

A catalogue for this title is available from the British Library.

ISBN 0-340-67935-2

First published 1997

Impression number   10 9 8 7 6 5 4 3 2 1
Year   1999   1998   1997

Copyright © 1997 Alan Farmer

Typeset by Sempringham publishing services, Bedford
Printed in Great Britain for Hodder & Stoughton Educational,
a division of Hodder Headline Plc, 338 Euston Road, London NW1 3BH
by Redwood Books, Trowbridge, Wiltshire

Contents

Preface

To the general reader

Although the *Access to History* series has been designed with the needs of students studying the subject at higher examination levels very much in mind, it also has a great deal to offer the general reader. The main body of the text (i.e. ignoring the Study Guides at the ends of chapters) forms a readable and yet stimulating survey of a coherent topic as studied by historians. However, each author's aim has not merely been to provide a clear explanation of what happened in the past (to interest and inform): it has also been assumed that most readers wish to be stimulated into thinking further about the topic and to form opinions of their own about the significance of the events that are described and discussed (to be challenged). Thus, although no prior knowledge of the topic is expected on the reader's part, she or he is treated as an intelligent and thinking person throughout. The author tends to share ideas and possibilities with the reader, rather than passing on numbers of so-called 'historical truths'.

To the student reader

There are many ways in which the series can be used by students studying History at a higher level. It will, therefore, be worthwhile thinking about your own study strategy before you start your work on this book. Obviously, your strategy will vary depending on the aim you have in mind, and the time for study that is available to you.

If, for example, you want to acquire a general overview of the topic in the shortest possible time, the following approach will probably be the most effective:

1 Read Chapter 1 and think about its contents.
2 Read the 'Making notes' section at the end of Chapter 2 and decide whether it is necessary for you to read this chapter.
3 If it is, read the chapter, stopping at each heading to note down the main points that have been made.
4 Repeat stage 2 (and stage 3 where appropriate) for all the other chapters.

If, however, your aim is to gain a thorough grasp of the topic, taking however much time is necessary to do so, you may benefit from carrying out the same procedure with each chapter, as follows:

1 Read the chapter as fast as you can, and preferably at one sitting.
2 Study the flow diagram at the end of the chapter, ensuring that you understand the general 'shape' of what you have just read.

3 Read the 'Making notes' section (and the 'Answering essay questions' section, if there is one) and decide what further work you need to do on the chapter. In particularly important sections of the book, this will involve reading the chapter a second time and stopping at each heading to think about (and to write a summary of) what you have just read.

4 Attempt the 'Source-based questions' section. It will sometimes be sufficient to think through your answers, but additional understanding will often be gained by forcing yourself to write them down.

When you have finished the main chapters of the book, study the 'Further Reading' section and decide what additional reading (if any) you will do on the topic.

This book has been designed to help make your studies both enjoyable and successful. If you can think of ways in which this could have been done more effectively, please write to tell me. In the meantime, I hope that you will gain greatly from your study of History.

Keith Randell

Acknowledgements

Cover - a portrait of Andrew Johnson, courtesy of Topham Picture Point.

Corbis (UK) Ltd. p. 108 (left and right) p. 131, p. 136, p. 137; Peter Newark's Western Americana pages p. 121; private collection p. 69, p. 75.

Every effort has been made to trace and acknowledge ownership of copyright. The Publishers will be glad to make suitable arrangements with any copyright holders whom it has not been possible to contact.

CHAPTER 1

The American Civil War

1 The Failure of the Great Experiment

Prior to 1861 the history of the United States had been in many ways a
remarkable success story. The small, predominantly English settlements
of the early seventeenth century had expanded rapidly, so much so that
by the end of the eighteenth century they had been able to win
independence from Britain. The USA, which in 1776 had only
controlled a narrow strip of land along the Atlantic seaboard, continued
to expand westwards. By 1850, largely as a result of the Louisiana
Purchase (1802-3), annexation of Texas (1845) and gains made after
success in the Mexican War (1846-8), the United States extended from
the Atlantic to the Pacific. By 1860 the original 13 states had increased
to 33. Many Americans thought it was their 'manifest destiny' to take
over the whole of North and Central America.

The country had also had considerable economic, social and political
success. By 1860 white Americans enjoyed a better standard of living
than any other people on earth. This prosperity and the rapidly
expanding economy attracted large-scale immigration. Before the 1840s
most immigrants to the USA had been British. In the 1840s and 1850s,
hundreds of thousands of Irish, Germans and Scandinavians poured
across the Atlantic. In 1860, 4,000,000 of America's 31,000,000 people
were foreign-born. The United States' political system, based on the
1787 Constitution, was the most modern in the world. Republican,
federal and democratic, it was the pride of most Americans and the envy
of most European radicals. By the mid-nineteenth century, the
American people were probably the most equal and certainly the best
educated in the world. Not surprisingly, many Americans considered
themselves to be the world's most civilised and fortunate people: in
novelist Henry Melville's view, 'The peculiar chosen people, the Israel
of our time'.

It should be said that not everyone benefited from what many
Americans saw as the 'great experiment'. During the 250 years that had
elapsed since the coming of the first English settlers, Native Americans
had lost most of their land. By 1860 only the Plains Indians still clung
precariously to their native land west of the Mississippi river. The other
major ethnic group that had not shared in the growing prosperity were
the African Americans, whose ancestors had been transported to
America as slaves. Although the slave trade had been declared illegal in
the USA in 1808, slavery itself continued in the American South. In
1860 there were some 4,000,000 slaves. This was a great anomaly in a
nation proud of the 1776 Declaration of Independence which stated that
'we hold these truths to be self-evident; that all men are created equal'.
In the opinion of many Northerners in 1860, the fact that slavery - 'the

peculiar institution' - still existed was the major failing of the 'great experiment'.

If slavery was the major failing of the great experiment pre-1860, the Civil War remains, without doubt, the greatest failure in American history. It represented an utter breakdown of the normal political processes. Political passions split the Union and as a result some 620,000 Americans were to die in the bloodiest war fought in the Western world between 1815 and 1914. The blood-letting was similar (proportionally) to that in Europe in the First World War. More Americans died in the Civil War than in all America's subsequent wars (to date) put together.

2 The Causes of the War

The causes of the Civil War have been - and continue to be - keenly debated. (For more detail on the causes, read the companion volume to this book, *The Origins of the American Civil War 1846-61*.) In March 1865 Abraham Lincoln declared that slavery was 'somehow' the cause of the war and, for half a century or so after the war, most historians agreed. In 1913, James Ford Rhodes, the foremost Civil War historian of his day, declared that 'of the American Civil War it may be safely asserted that there was a single cause, slavery'. But there were some historians at that time, and there have been many since, who disagreed strongly with this view. The Confederate leader Jefferson Davis insisted in his memoirs that the Southern states had seceded and gone to war not to protect slavery but to vindicate state sovereignty. Many Southerners accepted this explanation and continued to view the conflict as a war of Northern aggression against Southern rights.

In the 1920s so-called 'progressive' historians, like Charles Beard, saw clashes between interest groups and classes as the central theme of history. In their eyes the war was not primarily a contest between slavery and freedom. Instead it was a contest between plantation agriculture and industrialising capitalism. According to Beard, the real issues dividing Northern manufacturers from Southern planters were the tariff, government subsidies to transportation and manufacturing, and public land sales.

During the 1940s another interpretation, usually called 'revisionism', dominated the work of academic historians. Revisionist historians, like James Randall and Avery Craven, denied that sectional conflicts between North and South - whether over slavery, state rights, or industry versus agriculture - were genuinely divisive. In the opinion of the revisionists, far more united than divided the two sections. White Americans, North and South, shared the same language, legal system, political culture, religious values and a common heritage. Most also had similar racist views, accepting without question that African Americans were inferior to whites. In the eyes of the revisionists, the differences that separated North and South could and should have been accommodated peacefully. The Civil War, therefore, was not an irrepressible conflict, as earlier generations had called it, but 'The Repressible Conflict' as Craven titled one of his books. The war was brought on not by genuine issues but by extremists on both sides - rabble-rousing Yankee abolitionists and Southern 'fire-eaters' - who whipped up emotions and hatreds for their own partisan purposes. The passions they aroused got out of hand because blundering politicians failed to find a sensible compromise. The result, according to the revisionists, was a tragic, unnecessary war that accomplished nothing that could not have been achieved by negotiation. Of course, any compromise in 1861 would have left slavery in place. But revisionists argued that slavery would soon have died peacefully of natural causes.

Historiography, however, has now come full circle. Most historians today agree with Lincoln's assertion that slavery was 'somehow' the cause of the war. The state rights, progressive and revisionist schools are presently dormant if not actually dead. Most historians believe that slavery lay at the root of the antagonism. To say that 'only' slavery divided the North from the South is akin to saying that 'only' religion divides people in Northern Ireland today. Slavery was the sole institution not shared by North and South. The peculiar institution defined the South, permeating almost every aspect of its life. In 1858 a prominent, and relatively moderate, Northern politician, Senator William Seward, declared that the social systems of slave labour and free labour 'are more than incongruous - they are incompatible'. In Seward's opinion, the friction between them was 'an irreconcilable conflict between opposing and enduring forces, and it means that the United States must and will, sooner or later, become either entirely a slaveholding nation, or entirely a free-labour nation'. By 1860 most Southerners agreed with Seward that an irreconcilable conflict had split the country into two hostile cultures.

Slaves were the principal form of wealth in the South. The market value of the South's 4,000,000 slaves in 1860 was $3 billion - more than the value of land and cotton. Slave labour made it possible for the South to grow 75 per cent of the world's cotton, which in turn constituted half of all the USA's exports. But slavery was much more than an economic system. It was a means of maintaining racial control and white supremacy. Northern whites were also committed to white supremacy. But with 95 per cent of the nation's black population in the South, the North's scale of concern with this matter was so much greater as to constitute a different order of magnitude and create a very different set of social priorities. The economic, social and racial centrality of slavery to the Southern way of life focused the region's politics overwhelmingly in defence of the peculiar institution. Only 25 per cent of Southern white families actually owned slaves in 1860. But the vast majority of non-slaveholding whites supported the peculiar institution. Many aspired to become slaveholders themselves. Most feared what would happen if the slaves were freed. By the mid-nineteenth century most Southerners saw slavery as a positive good - essential to the peace, safety and prosperity of the South.

Southerners were provoked into defending their peculiar institution by the rise of militant abolitionism in the North after 1830. William Lloyd Garrison, Frederick Douglass and a host of other eloquent crusaders branded slavery as inhumane, a sin, and a violation of the republican principles of liberty on which the USA had been founded. Although the radical abolitionists did not win much support in the North with their message of racial equality, the belief that slavery was unjust, obsolete and unrepublican entered mainstream Northern politics and Northerners increasingly extolled the virtues of a free-labour ideology.

It was the issue of the expansion of slavery, rather than its existence, that polarised the nation. Most of the crises that threatened the bonds of Union arose over this matter. The first one, in 1819-20, was settled by the Missouri Compromise. The annexation of the huge slave state of Texas in 1845 provoked new tensions. It also provoked war with Mexico in 1846 which resulted in American acquisition of 750,000 square miles of new territory. This opened a Pandora's box of troubles. Convinced that the 'Slave Power' in Washington had engineered the annexation of Texas and the Mexican War, Northerners struck back. In 1846 Congressman David Wilmot introduced a resolution banning slavery in all territories that might be conquered from Mexico. Wilmot's Proviso passed the House of Representatives (where the larger Northern population gave the free states a majority) but failed to pass the Senate (where the South had equal representation). The most ominous feature of the Wilmot Proviso was its wrenching of the normal pattern of party divisions. After 1846 sectional voting became the norm on any issue concerning slavery. Southerners, worried by Northern growth, increasingly accepted the views of John C. Calhoun and claimed that sovereignty lay in the individual states. According to Calhoun, secession might well be a justified process if slavery was threatened.

Despite the fact that the Northern population was much greater than that of the South, Southerners managed to preserve the appearance of political power. This happened because the South usually controlled the Democrat Party, which in turn usually controlled the government. The Democrat Party continued to win considerable support in the North, largely from immigrant Irish and German Catholics and from farmers (often of Southern stock) in Mid-Western states like Illinois. Southern domination of the Democrat Party increased during the 1850s. Although the Democrat Presidents Franklin Pierce (1853-7) and James Buchanan (1857-61) were Northerners, they held pro-Southern views.

This - unnatural - Southern political dominance convinced many Northerners that there really was a Slave Power conspiracy at work, subverting the nation's values and institutions. This fear helped give birth to the Republican Party - a purely Northern party - committed to opposing both the Slave Power and slavery expansion. Republicans carried most Northern states in the 1856 presidential election. But Democrat James Buchanan, who won a handful of Northern states and virtually all the Southern states, became President. However, his pro-Southern policies (particularly in Kansas) resulted in a split in the Democrat Party. By 1858 many Northern Democrats, following the lead of Senator Stephen Douglas of Illinois, broke with Buchanan. In 1860 Northern Democrats nominated Douglas for President. Southern Democrats nominated John Breckinridge. This helped ensure the election of the Republican candidate Abraham Lincoln. Lincoln won virtually no Southern votes but carried every Northern state.

For many Southerners, Lincoln's election was the writing on the wall. It seemed they had lost control of the government. The fact that the North had elected a President who believed slavery a 'monstrous injustice' that should be 'placed in the course of ultimate extinction' seemed both a threat and an affront to Southern honour. So, even though the Republicans lacked a majority in either house of Congress, seven lower South states voted to secede from the Union. South Carolina was the first to go in December 1860. Mississippi, Florida, Alabama, Georgia, Louisiana and Texas soon followed. Delegates from these states met at Montgomery, Alabama, in February 1861 and formed the Confederacy. Jefferson Davis was elected Confederate President.

However, eight upper South slave states did not immediately secede. Less committed to slavery than the lower South, many in the upper South hoped for a compromise that would preserve the Union. But no room for compromise could be found. Lincoln and the Republicans were committed to preventing slavery expansion: the Confederate states were committed to going their own way.

Secession did not necessarily mean war. Lincoln's government could have allowed the 'erring sisters' to depart in peace. But Lincoln, like most Northerners, was not willing to accept the dismemberment of the USA. Most Northerners realised that toleration of disunion would end the great experiment in republican self-government. It would create a precedent to be invoked by disaffected minorities in the future. Even President Buchanan regarded secession as illegal. But, as a 'lame duck' President after November 1860, he was not prepared to do anything about it. Lincoln, however, made it abundantly clear in his inaugural address in March 1861, that he was determined to maintain the Union. He hoped to keep the eight upper South slave states in the Union and to persuade the lower South states to return by assurances that he had no intention of interfering with slavery in states where it already existed.

Lincoln, who had hoped that time would allow passions to cool, found himself facing an immediate crisis. In his inaugural speech, he had pledged himself to maintain Fort Sumter, situated on an island in Charleston harbour. Confederate President Davis, like many Southerners, considered it dishonourable that the Union flag was still flying off one of the Confederacy's main harbours. When Lincoln decided to resupply the garrison which was running short of food, Davis determined to assert Confederate sovereignty. When the Union commander of Fort Sumter refused to surrender, Confederate troops opened fire on 12 April, 1861, forcing the Union garrison to surrender. Lincoln immediately called upon those states remaining in the Union for troops. The upper South states now had to commit themselves. Virginia, Tennessee, Arkansas and North Carolina voted to join the Confederacy. Maryland, Missouri, Delaware and (eventually) Kentucky committed themselves to the Union. By the summer of 1861 the USA was divided North against South.

In 1861 Lincoln was not pledged to end slavery: he was pledged to preserve the Union. The Confederate states were fighting for the right to self-determination. Thus nationalism became the central issue of the struggle on both sides. Historians continue to debate the extent to which the South had a national identity in 1861. By the mid-nineteenth century, there were certainly some Southerners who fervently believed in a separate Southern destiny. However, before 1860 there had been little enthusiasm for creating a Southern nation. Most Southerners had seen themselves as loyal Americans. The Southern 'fire-eaters'/ nationalists were a small minority. They did not obtain high office either before - or indeed after - 1861. Most Southerners considered them cranks and fanatics. Many of those who advocated secession during the winter of 1860-1 did so reluctantly. The establishment of the Confederacy was a refuge to which many Southerners felt driven, not a national destiny that they eagerly embraced. But, perceiving slavery to be under threat, they voted to leave the Union. Slavery, therefore, underpinned the nationalist struggle. It was the obvious difference between the two sections. It made the South distinct. It was the main reason for the growth of sectionalism. No other issue could have led to the disruption of the Union.

3 Southern Blame

Throughout the Civil War - and for many years afterwards - Northerners blamed Southerners for the war and Southerners blamed Northerners. In the mid-twentieth century 'revisionist' historians were quite happy to mete out blame and were reasonably even-handed in so doing, castigating fanatics and bigots in both sections. On balance, though, the revisionists tended to focus most of their criticism on Northern anti-slavery radicals who continually attacked 'the peculiar institution' and the South as a whole - thus goading Southerners into a defensive response. More recently, historians have largely eschewed the notion of 'blame', preferring instead simply to explain how and why the Civil War occurred. It is impossible, however, for historians to take a totally objective stance and to avoid judgement. With hindsight it seems obvious that Southern politicians did blunder into war in 1861. However, it would be wrong simply to condemn Southern politicians. For the most part, the politicians represented the views of their constituents. Unfortunately, most Southerners were swept by an irrational tide of emotion after Lincoln's election success in November 1860. As a result, Southerners embarked on a course of action that was always likely to lead to war - and a war that Southerners were always very likely to lose. The likely results of secession - and war - were apparent to many Southerners - and most Northerners - in 1861. It is thus fair to point the finger of blame at the Confederate leaders and their supporters.

There are many similarities between the actions of the South in 1861 and the actions of Japan in 1941. Both the Southerners and the Japanese felt that they had been pushed into a corner from which there was no honourable escape. Honour replaced reason. Both the Confederate states and Japan closed their eyes to the likely outcome of their actions. Both actually fired the first shots of the war - the Confederates at Fort Sumter in April 1861: the Japanese at Pearl Harbor in December 1941. By so doing they succeeded in provoking conflict and uniting against them the whole of the USA in 1941 and what remained of the USA in 1861. Winston Churchill commented in December 1941 that the Japanese, by attacking Britain and the USA, had embarked on a 'very considerable undertaking'. The same could be said of the South's decision to go to war with the North in 1861. As a result of a series of blunders, one in four white male Southerners of military age died: the South's profitable economy was devastated; and slavery - the institution which the South had gone to war to defend and which was not under any immediate threat in 1861 - ended.

4 Northern Victory

Efforts to explain Northern victory and Southern defeat have generated a great deal of historical controversy. The debate began almost as soon as the war ended and still continues. Today most historians acknowledge the fact that there were many causes for Southern defeat/Northern victory. However, historians still tend to emphasise one or two causes at the expense of others. Some focus mainly or entirely on the Confederacy and usually ask 'Why did the Confederacy lose?'. Others, concentrating on the North, ask 'Why did the Union win?'.

In 1861 most Southerners and most European observers were confident that the Confederacy would triumph. Even after the war, many prominent Southerners were convinced that the Confederacy should have won. The sheer size of the Confederacy - 750,000 square miles - was perhaps its greatest asset. Twice the size of the original 13 colonies, it would obviously be difficult to blockade and conquer. Unlike the Union, the Confederacy did not have to invade, capture and hold down hostile territory. All it needed to do was defend. Defence, in both strategic and tactical terms, is usually an easier option in war than attack. The Union had little option but to attack. There was no other way it could win the war. Southerners hoped that Northern public opinion might come to question high losses. If Northern will collapsed, the Confederacy would win by default.

The Confederacy also appeared to have important psychological advantages. Given that most of the war was fought within the Confederacy, Southerners were defending their own land and homes - a fact that perhaps encouraged them to fight that much harder than Northerners who were fighting for the more abstract pursuit of reunion. Morale, commitment and enthusiasm for war were high in the South in 1861. Most Southerners were convinced that man for man they were far better soldiers than Northerners. In 1861 most contemporary observers agreed that in terms of familiarity with weapons, emphasis on martial virtues, and military training, the South had important advantages. Southerners had fought superbly well in the Mexican War and before that in the war for Texan independence. From the American War of Independence onwards, the elite of the nation's generals had all been Southerners. The fact that many Northerners feared that Southerners were indeed better soldiers also ensured that the Confederacy began the war with a psychological advantage - an advantage which was enhanced by the Confederacy winning the first major battle at Manassas.

'King Cotton' was assumed to be the Confederacy's great economic weapon. It was expected that cotton sales would enable the Confederacy to purchase weapons and supplies from Europe. There was also the possibility that Britain might break the Union naval blockade to ensure that cotton supplies got through to its textile mills. This might well lead to war between Britain and the Union. If the Confederacy won British support, there was every chance it would win independence.

Despite these advantages the Confederacy lost. Why? Some historians have explained Confederate defeat by · claiming the Confederacy was badly led. They have blamed both political leaders (especially Jefferson Davis) and military leaders (including Robert E. Lee). However, to blame a few leaders for the South's defeat is far too simplistic. In many ways it is fairer to praise Southern leaders than to blame them. It is difficult to think of a Confederate leader who could have done a better job than Davis. It is impossible to think of a better general than Lee. Despite being outnumbered in every major battle and campaign in which he fought, he won victories - which gave Southerners hope, dampened spirits in the North and impressed European political leaders. Without Lee's generalship, the Confederacy would have crumbled earlier.

Other historians have explained Confederate defeat by focusing on divisions within the South. There are several variations on this theme. Some think that the notion of state rights crippled the efforts of Davis's government to wage war. Individual states are seen as putting their own interests before those of the Confederacy. But recent scholarship has shown that the negative effects of state rights sentiment have been much exaggerated. Rather than hindering the efforts of the Confederate government, the activities of states augmented them. A variant of the state rights thesis focuses on the resistance by many Southerners to such war measures as conscription, direct taxation and martial law. Opponents denounced these measures on grounds of civil liberties, state rights, or democratic individualism, or all three combined. According to David Donald, insistence on preserving democratic practices so weakened the Confederate war effort that the inscription on the Confederacy's tombstone should read: 'Died of Democracy'. This claim is not convincing. During the war, Davis's government suppressed dissent and suspended civil liberties as thoroughly as did Lincoln's government. The Confederacy enacted conscription a year before the Union and raised a larger proportion of its troops by drafting than did the North.

Recent scholarship has stressed that many groups within the South, especially the non-slaveholding yeoman farmers, became increasingly disenchanted as the war progressed, believing it was 'a rich man's war and a poor man's fight'. Two thirds of the Confederacy's white population were non-slaveholders. Some of them, especially in upland regions, had opposed secession in 1861. Others, who initially supported the Confederacy, possibly became alienated as the war caused increasing hardship. There may have been a growing suspicion that they were risking their lives and property simply to defend slavery - and slaveholders. A conviction of class discrimination and social injustice may have damaged Confederate unity. However, it is easy to exaggerate the extent of internal alienation. Large numbers of non-slaveholding Southerners were ready to fight and die for the Confederate cause from start to finish of the war.

Another major explanation for Confederate defeat holds that the Confederacy could have won if the Southern people had possessed the will to make the sacrifices necessary for victory. The lack-of-will thesis has four main facets. The first - and main - argument is that the Confederacy, given its short existence, did not generate a strong sense of nationalism and Southerners, therefore, did not have as firm a conviction as Northerners of fighting for a country. It is thus claimed that when the going got tough, Southerners found it tough to keep going. If the nationalist spirit had been strong enough, it is argued, the Confederacy could have continued the fight after 1865. But Southerners' desire for independence was insufficient to support a savage guerrilla war. This argument, it should be said, is not convincing. Southerners fought hard and long for their cause and suffered terrible casualties. Far from being a reason for defeat, the strength of Southern nationalism explains why most Southerners fought as long and as hard as they did. Southerners persisted through far greater hardship and suffering than that experienced most Northerners. Southerners persisted through far greater hardship and suffering than that experienced by most Northerners. In the summer of 1864 Northerners almost threw in the towel when they suffered casualty rates that Southerners had endured for more than two years. The Confederacy endured a death toll far greater than France's in the Franco-Prussian War (1870-1). Nobody seriously suggests that Frenchmen in 1870 did not have a strong sense of national identity. Yet France lost. Strong nationalism is not a magic shield ensuring invulnerability to those who possess it.

The second lack-of-will interpretation - the notion that many Southern whites felt moral qualms about slavery, which undermined their will to fight a war to preserve it - is even less convincing. Most white Southerners went to war to preserve their peculiar institution and remained committed to it to the end: it was the chief reason why they fought and died for four terrible years.

A third lack-of-will interpretation focuses on religion. At the outset most Southerners believed they were fighting a just war. But as the war went on and the South suffered so much death and destruction, it is argued that Southerners came to doubt whether God was really on their side and that this helped corrode Confederate morale. This viewpoint is hard to substantiate. Most Southerners seem to have had few doubts about the justice of their cause. Over the winter of 1863-4 a great religious revival movement swept through the Confederate army. Rather than explaining Confederate defeat, religion played a vital role in actually sustaining Southern will.

The final lack-of-will argument concentrates on the economic and financial situation. In 1861 the Confederacy was far from self-sufficient: it was dependent on the North and Britain for most of its manufactured goods. The Northern blockade meant that by 1862 there was a shortage of almost everything. The inability of the Confederate states to maintain the railroad system worsened the economic situation. The effects of runaway inflation, brought about by shortages and the issue of huge quantities of paper money, were devastating. Severe hardship on the home front led, it is claimed, to a slow but relentless growth of defeatism which was conveyed by uncensored letters to Confederate soldiers. Women wanted their sons and husbands home and told them to put family before national loyalty. By 1864-5 many Confederate soldiers, suffering from terrible shortages themselves, simply left the ranks and went home. There is some truth in this economic hardship argument. However, there is a significant difference between loss and lack of will. A people whose armies are beaten, railroads wrecked, cities burned, countryside occupied and crops laid waste, quite naturally lose their will to continue fighting. This is what happened to the Confederacy. It was Union military success which created war weariness and which destroyed morale. By 1865 the Confederacy had lost its will for sacrifice. But it was military defeat which caused the loss of will, not lack of will which caused military defeat.

In reality, the Confederacy fought better than might have been expected. The reason for Northern victory lies in the North. To win, the Confederacy had to wear down Northern will. A long, bloody war was the best way to do this. The war was long and bloody but Northern will endured. There were a variety of reasons for this. There was a great sense of American nationalism in 1861. Hundreds of thousands of Northern men were prepared to fight and die to preserve the Union. Strong leadership at every level, from Lincoln downwards, had some effect. The fact that the Northern economy was able to produce both 'guns' and 'butter' helped civilian morale. For many Northern families life during the war went on much the same as usual. The North was never seriously invaded and, despite higher taxes, many Northerners experienced increased prosperity as the war progressed. But ultimately Northern will, like Southern will, seems to have been crucially effected by the outcome of campaigns and battles.

The reason why - ultimately - the North won the war was because it won campaigns and battles. It did so because it had more men and resources. The historian Richard Current, reviewing the statistics of Northern demographic and economic preponderance - two and a half times the South's population, three times its railroad capacity, nine times its industrial production, overwhelming naval supremacy - concluded that 'surely in view of the disparity of resources, it would have taken a miracle ... to enable the South to win. As usual, God was on the side of the heaviest battalions'. More recently Shelby Foote declared: 'the North fought that war with one hand behind its back'. If necessary, 'the North simply would have brought that other arm from behind its back. I don't think the South ever had a chance to win that war.'

History does offer examples of societies winning wars against greater odds than the Confederacy faced. The outstanding example in the minds of everyone in 1861 was the United States' own victory in its War of Independence against Britain. Superior strategy, leadership and morale can be more important than superior numbers and resources. But in war larger and better equipped armies do normally triumph. The Civil War was to be no exception. After a savage bloodbath, Southern will finally collapsed while Northern will held. If Confederate armies had continued to have had the same success on the battlefield as in the first two years of the war, it is unlikely that Southern morale would have collapsed. In the event Union armies from mid-1863 onwards won the main battles. The principal reason for this was not so much better leadership but the fact that Union armies were larger and better equipped. General Ulysses Grant in 1864-5 used the immense advantage of Northern numbers and military resources to good effect. Those advantages had always been there: the Union just needed someone to ensure that they were applied steadily and remorselessly. Grant did just that. Unable to fight a perfect war, the Confederacy fell before the superior resources of the enemy.

5 The Emancipation of the Slaves

From start to finish Lincoln's main aim was to preserve the Union. In September 1862 he proclaimed: 'If I could save the Union without freeing any slaves I would do it, and if I could save it by freeing all the slaves, I would do it, and if I could save it by freeing some and leaving others alone I would also do that'. Lincoln was articulating the view of most Northerners. For Northerners, the most important result of the war was, not that slaves were freed but, that the Union survived.

Only gradually did the war to save the Union become a war to free the slave. From start to finish many Northern Democrats fought simply to restore the Union and opposed freeing slaves. In 1861 most Republicans were also reluctant to support emancipation as an overt war aim. Moderate Republicans, including Abraham Lincoln, were aware that it was essential to preserve Northern unity. They were also aware that there was strong racial prejudice in the North. Many Northerners feared that freed slaves might head North, with disastrous results. There were other fears. An avowed policy of freeing the slaves would probably spur Southerners to an even greater effort and leave no possibility of a compromise peace. A pro-emancipation policy would also alienate the four slave states which remained within the Union - Kentucky, Maryland, Missouri and Delaware. Together, these states had some 400,000 slaves.

In consequence, to the dismay of abolitionists, both Congress and Lincoln tackled the slavery issue with great caution in the first months of the war. Although Lincoln had long considered slavery a moral evil, he declared in April 1861 that 'I have no purpose, directly or indirectly, to interfere with the institution of slavery in the States where it exists. I believe I have no lawful right to do so, and I have no inclination to do so'. Congress supported this stance. In July 1861 it adopted the Crittenden resolutions disclaiming any intention of meddling with 'the rights or established institutions' of the South (i.e. slavery). These resolutions won overwhelming Congressional approval.

But as the months went by and it became increasingly clear that there was little likelihood of the Confederate states being enticed back into the Union, so-called radical Republicans, many of whom had sat in Congress for many years, began to make their influence felt. To many radicals, it seemed that to fight slaveholders without fighting against slavery, was (in Frederick Douglass's words) a 'half-hearted business'. Given their prestige, skill and energy, many radicals found themselves in control of key committees in both the Senate (where Charles Sumner chaired the Committee on Foreign Relations) and in the House (where Thaddeus Stevens chaired the powerful Committee on Ways and Means). Most radicals were genuinely concerned for black Americans. Virtually all had a loathing of white slaveholders who they blamed for causing the war. All were concerned that if the Union was restored without slavery being abolished, nothing would have been solved. Radicals, almost without exception, believed that measures to emancipate slaves would weaken the Southern war effort. Slaves would become a fifth column in the South. Many would flee to the North, weakening the South and strengthening the Northern cause. Finally, if emancipation became a Northern war aim there was little chance that Britain would support the Confederacy. 'It is often said that war will make an end of Slavery,' declared Sumner in October 1861. 'This is probable. But it is surer still that the overthrow of Slavery will make an end of the war.' By the time Congress re-convened in December 1861, most Republican Congressmen supported a tougher stand against slavery. The Crittenden resolutions were forgotten. Month by month Congress passed anti-slavery measures (26 in all). Most Republicans accepted that Congress had no authority to end slavery by a simple act. Only a constitutional amendment could do that. However, Lincoln, using his war-time powers, could take action. Congressmen, in consequence, began to put pressure on Lincoln.

Lincoln was determined to keep personal control of the emancipation issue. For several months, anxious about the border states and determined to maintain Northern unity, he seemed to prevaricate. In July 1862, the abolitionist Garrison described the President's handling of the slavery issue as 'stumbling, halting, prevaricating, irresolute, weak, besotted.'. However, by mid-1862 Lincoln was convinced that a bold step was necessary. He was aware of Congressional opinion. But his main conviction was that a bold statement on emancipation would weaken the Confederacy. Military necessity dominated his thoughts in the depressing summer of 1862. He finally issued his Emancipation Proclamation in September 1862. On the surface the Proclamation seemed to be extremely cautious. Slavery was to be left untouched in states that returned to the Union before January 1863. Thereafter all slaves in enemy territory conquered by Union armies would be 'forever free'. The Proclamation, therefore, had no effect whatsoever on slavery in loyal Union states like Kentucky. It did not even effect slavery in those parts of Louisiana, Virginia and Tennessee which had already been brought back under Union control. Nevertheless, most radicals were delighted at what they saw as a bold act on Lincoln's part. They appreciated that Lincoln had gone as far as his powers allowed in making the war a war to end slavery. They also appreciated that the Emancipation Proclamation added a moral dimension to the conflict. As Union forces advanced, slavery in the South would end. Once slavery had ended in the South, it could not possibly survive in the border states. According to the historian Richard Ransom, 'With the stroke of a pen, the president had turned the war into a revolution'.

Most Northern Democrats saw it this way and disliked what they saw. Claiming that Lincoln had unwisely and unconstitutionally changed the war's objective from reunion to abolition, Democrat politicians vehemently denounced the Proclamation. and made it a central issue in the 1862 mid-term elections. Undeterred by Democrat opposition (and some election success), Lincoln went ahead with his promise and on 1 January 1863 proclaimed that the freedom of all slaves in rebellious regions was now a Union war aim - 'an act of justice' as well as a 'military necessity'. Not wishing to be held responsible for a bloody slave revolt, he urged slaves 'to abstain from all violence, unless in necessary self-defence'. But at the same time, he called on Union forces to protect the rights of those they made free.

Jefferson Davis condemned the Proclamation as 'the most execrable measure recorded in the history of guilty man'. The Confederacy could no longer look for a compromise settlement. If it was going to protect its peculiar institution, it must fight to the bitter end. In the short term, the Emancipation Proclamation may well have helped to stiffen Confederate resistance, as Lincoln had feared. However, in the long term, the Confederacy was undoubtedly weakened by Lincoln's emancipation policy. The Confederacy's hopes of gaining recognition abroad were dashed for good. By encouraging slaves to flee to Union lines, the Proclamation worsened an already serious manpower shortage within the Confederacy.

In 1861 and well into 1862 Lincoln had faced strong and conflicting pressure on the question of whether or not to enlist blacks in the Union army. Abolitionists were anxious that blacks should fight in a war that was likely to weaken if not destroy slavery. But initially most Northerners opposed black recruitment. Many hated the notion of blacks fighting with and against other whites and doubted that blacks would make good soldiers. Lincoln stood firm against black recruitment for the first year of the war. But after the Emancipation Proclamation, Lincoln's resistance to enlisting black soldiers abated and from the spring of 1863 onwards there was a large influx of black troops into the Union army. As in so many respects, the President was in tune with Northern public opinion. With casualty lists mounting and white recruitment falling off, Lincoln knew there was far more support for black soldiers than there had been in 1861. Of the 46,000 free blacks of military age in the North, some 33,000 joined the Union armies. The majority of black troops, however, were ex-slaves. Some 100,000 were recruited from the Confederate states. Another 42,000 slaves from Kentucky, Delaware, Maryland and Missouri also enlisted in the Union army. (This was the swiftest way for border state slaves to get their freedom.) By 1865 some

180,000 blacks had served in the Union army.

Within the Union army there was considerable racial discrimination. Black and white regiments were strictly segregated. Black regiments were invariably commanded by white officers. By 1865 scarcely 100 black soldiers had become officers and there were none above the rank of captain. Black regiments usually received inferior supplies and equipment. What rankled most, however, was the fact that there were pay differentials: black privates received only $10 a month while white privates received $13. Not until June 1864 did Congress at last agree to provide equal pay for blacks.

Although Sherman was reluctant to use black troops in the West, they played an important role in the fighting around Petersburg and Richmond in 1864-5. Most black regiments seem to have fought as well as white regiments. There may have been a tendency recently to exaggerate the impact black soldiers had on the outcome of the war. Of the 37,000 black soldiers who died in the war, only 3,000 actually died in combat. Black soldiers only fought at the end: they did not take part in the crucial battles of 1863. But nevertheless there seems little doubt that the influx of black troops had a positive effect on the Union war effort at a critical time. By 1865 there were nearly as many black soldiers in arms against the Confederacy as there were white soldiers defending it. Black participation in the war was also important in bolstering black confidence and race pride. Moreover, military service carried with it an assumption of American citizenship. The black abolitionist leader Frederick Douglass commented: 'Once let the black man get upon his person the brass letters US, let him get an eagle on his buttons and musket on his shoulder ... and there is no power on earth which can deny that he has earned the right to citizenship in the United States.'

As late as 1864 Lincoln's Proclamation was the only formal evidence of Northern commitment to emancipation. Given that the Proclamation was an executive order that would have questionable force once the war ended, the Republicans determined to extend the basis of emancipation by passing a constitutional amendment to end slavery. In April 1864 the Senate passed the amendment but Democrats in the House opposed the measure and prevented it from receiving the two-thirds support needed. In June 1864 Lincoln urged the Republican national convention meeting at Baltimore 'to put into the platform as the key stone' a plank endorsing a constitutional amendment to end slavery. The convention did as he asked. Interpreting his election success in November 1864 as a mandate for the anti-slavery amendment, Lincoln redoubled his efforts to secure Congressional approval and applied patronage pressure to a number of Democrats in the House - to considerable effect. On 31 January 1865 the House approved (with 3 votes to spare) the Thirteenth Amendment for ratification by the states. The radical Thaddeus Stevens remarked that, 'The greatest measure of the 19th century was passed by corruption, aided and abetted by the purest man in America'. Lincoln was delighted that the amendment was passed. He announced it was 'a King's cure for all the evils. It winds the whole thing up'.

It hardly did that. The problem of race relations after the war was likely to be difficult. Most Northerners did not concede that blacks and whites were equal and there was still massive segregation across the North. Lincoln himself was doubtful if the white and black races could live peacefully together. For most of the war slavery continued to operate in the four Northern border states. Maryland finally abolished slavery in October 1864 and Missouri followed in early 1865. But in Kentucky and Delaware slavery actually survived the Civil War. (It remained legal in Kentucky until December 1865 - eight months after the war was over.) The situation in the South was likely to be even more complex. What would happen to the 4,000,000 or so emancipated slaves remained to be seen.

6 The Impact of the Civil War

Many Northerners in the years after 1865 were positive about the Civil War. They felt they had fought for a just cause and extolled the fact that that cause had triumphed. Oliver Wendell Holmes, a Union soldier who later became one of America's great judges, treasured the war as a time when the nation had seen 'the snowy heights of honour ... above the goldfields'. Ex-slaves held similar positive views: most saw the winning of freedom as the watershed of their lives. Naturally enough, white Southerners did not view the war quite so positively. One, Edmund Ruffin, thought the Confederacy's defeat so disastrous that in June 1865 he shot himself, proclaiming, in the last words in his diary, 'unmitigated hatred to Yankee rule'. However, as time passed and the memories of the bitterness of defeat faded, white Southerners increasingly saw the war as a romantic 'Lost Cause' in which they had fought the good fight and come close to victory.

Some historians, however, appalled by the 620,000 deaths, have continued to question whether the war was worth fighting. The historian Merton Cooper was adamant: 'The Civil War was not worth the cost...What good the war produced would have come with time in an orderly way; the bad would not have come at all'. Most historians, however, have held - and continue to hold - far more positive views: the Union after all, was saved and 4,000,000 slaves were freed. Many regard the Civil War as 'The' event which helped define modern America. The historian/writer Shelby Foote saw the war as a watershed: before the war, he thought, the collection of 'United' States were an 'are': after the war the USA became an 'is'. (Foote might have added that during the war, it seemed possible that the USA might well become a 'was'!) Some historians regard the Civil War as the second American revolution. (The first revolution was the war of American Independence.) Many of those who lived through the war would have concurred with this view: most shared a common sense of having lived through events that had radically changed their world.

The war certainly had an immediate and colossal impact on both North and South. In 1865 much of the South was devastated: equipment and buildings were destroyed; the South's transportation system was in ruins; and there had been a 30-40 per cent reduction in Southern horses, mules, cattle and sheep. More important, one quarter of the South's male population of military age had been killed. This was likely to have massive economic and social effects. So too was the fact that slavery had been abolished. A new kind of labour system would need to replace it.

The war had other implications. Arguably it effectively changed the whole emphasis of the constitution, shifting the balance of the federal system in a national direction at the expense of state rights. The defeat of the Confederacy was a defeat of those who held extreme state rights' views. The war had also resulted in the federal government in Washington asserting its power in ways unimaginable in 1861. It had mobilised hundreds of thousands of men into the Union armed forces. To help pay for the war effort, the federal government had been forced to interfere in a host of economic and financial matters. It had raised tariffs and levied new sources of revenue including the income tax. It had set up a national bank and issued a national paper currency - greenbacks. Lincoln's administration, on occasions, had ridden roughshod over state and individual liberties. Many also felt that the President had ridden roughshod over the rights of Congress and the Supreme Court. During the war, Lincoln, as Commander-in Chief, had played a major role, using his (ill-defined) war powers creatively and extensively.

It was not only presidential power which had increased. Some historians think that the power of American big business had increased even more. The new financial system which emerged in the war - greenbacks, bonds, high taxes and a national banking system - may have helped promote large scale industrial enterprise. The war may also have had major effects on the Northern economy. Some claim it gave a stimulus to new methods of production, organisation and marketing. Perhaps it forced manufacturers and traders to think more than ever in terms of a national market. The war may well have brought about a redistribution of income in favour of the manufacturing interests in general and of the North-eastern region of the USA in particular.

However, it is all too easy to exaggerate the catalytic effects of the Civil War. Although the South suffered extensive devastation in the war, it was essentially an agrarian society. Land is rarely permanently damaged by military action. The damage could be - and indeed was - quickly repaired after 1865. The re-building of the Southern infrastructure was likely to encourage economic activity. The South could hope for capital investment from the North. Now the war was over it could also sell its cotton again. Given that cotton was in short supply in

1865, Southern farmers could expect good prices. The slaves were freed. But little had been done in the war to define and guarantee the position of African Americans in American society. White Southerners still hoped to control black labour and use it to produce cotton, tobacco, sugar and hemp. Except for a handful of radicals, few Republican politicians in 1865 advocated the confiscation and wholesale redistribution of Southern land. Lincoln seems to have given this matter little attention. His hope was to reintegrate the defeated South back into the Union as quickly as possible. In consequence, he had no wish to antagonise white Southerners. Ex-slaves, in consequence, were unlikely to have the means to improve their economic, social and political status.

So many of the functions assumed by the federal government during the war were clearly exceptional and justified only by the unique circumstances of the war. The rapid demobilisation of the North's armed forces after May 1865 was an obvious example of the hasty abandonment of the federal government's wartime powers. Individual states had played an important role in the war and were likely to play a more important role than the federal government in most Americans' lives after 1865. Nor had the war necessarily effected the relationship between the executive and the legislative branches of government. Once the war ended the President was no longer Commander-in-Chief. His powers were thus greatly reduced.

To argue that the Civil War transferred effective economic and political power into the hands of industrial capitalism is simplistic and over-dramatic. American business was no single monolithic interest engaged in a giant conspiracy to exploit the war for its own ends. It contained a variety of often conflicting interests which disagreed with each other over many financial and economic matters. If the big manufacturers proved to be the chief economic beneficiaries of the war (and this is debatable) their victory was an incidental rather a planned result of the conflict. It is doubtful if the war brought about any major economic changes in the North which would not otherwise have occurred.

Had the South won, the Civil War would undoubtedly have been one of the great turning points in modern history. Indeed, the long-term implications of a Confederate victory for both America and the world are so far reaching as to be incalculable. But Union victory meant in effect that a potential revolution by the 'radical right' of the day was crushed. The status quo was preserved. Preservation of the status quo does not sound very revolutionary. While it is possible to argue that the maintenance of the status quo resulted in the greatest remodelling which the Union has ever known, it is just as easy to claim that the Civil War scarcely effected the deeper currents of economic, social and political development in America.

Whether the results of the war were indeed revolutionary is the central issue of the rest of this book. To what extent did the outcome of the war effect white Southerners? To what extent did it effect black Southerners? To what extent did it effect the economic, social and political developments in the North? To what extent did it effect Western expansion? In short, was it America's second revolution?

Working on *'The American Civil War'*

This chapter has four main objectives: to give you an understanding of the causes of the Civil War; to make you aware that historians have different views about why the North won/South lost; to give you some notion of the way the war affected the lot of African Americans; and to briefly consider the impact of the war on American political, economic and social life. As you read the following chapters, you must try to judge whether the Civil War did indeed have a revolutionary impact on America's development. Was it a spectacular watershed in America's history? Or was it a mere bump on the surface of America's overall progression?

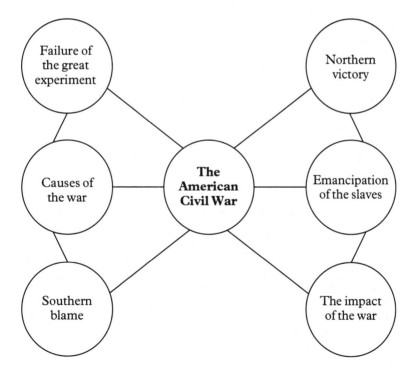

Summary - The American Civil War

CHAPTER 2

The Problem of Reconstruction, 1865-8

1 Introduction

In 1865 the triumphant federal government faced the problem of making peace and restoring the eleven former Confederate states to the Union. This process is known as reconstruction. The period from 1865 to 1877 is often called the 'age of reconstruction'. However, the chronological definition of reconstruction is a matter of some dispute. To begin with, reconstruction was not something which began in 1865: it was an issue from April 1861 onwards; it was really what the war was all about. Nor did the process of reconstruction necessarily end with the so-called Compromise of 1877. (In most states it ended much earlier!) The debate over time-scale is by no means the only debate about reconstruction. Virtually every aspect of the topic is - and has been - the subject of intense controversy.

If reconstructing 'reconstruction' is hard for historians, the reality of reconstruction was an even more intractable problem for American politicians at the time. There were no precedents and the Constitution provided little guidance. There were also fundamental disagreements about the basic issue of bringing the seceded states back into the Union. Ironically, the former Confederate states, which had happily seceded in 1861, now claimed they had never legally been out of the Union. Equally ironically, many Northern Republicans, who had insisted the Southern states could not secede, now claimed that they had in fact seceded, thereby reverting to territorial status! There were other important matters to be resolved. Somehow a feeling of loyalty to the Union had to be restored among white Southerners. Somehow the war-torn economy of the South had to be rebuilt. And somehow the newly-freed slaves (usually called 'freedmen') had to be given the opportunity to enjoy their new freedom.

Historians have long debated whether reconstruction was a success or a tragic failure. In the early part of the twentieth century, white Southern historians (such as Professor W.A. Dunning) usually claimed that the Confederate states had been cruelly oppressed. Reconstruction was seen as 'The Tragic Era' and 'The Age of Hate' - a dreadful time when the South was 'put to the torture': when Southerners suffered military occupation: when the South was ruled by incompetent and corrupt governments; and when blacks, unprepared for freedom, proved incapable of properly exercising the political rights which the North thrust upon them. Professor Dunning had no doubts who were the heroes: President Andrew Johnson who fought to continue the aims of Abraham Lincoln; white Southern Democrats who waged a forceful campaign to 'redeem' the South; and their allies - the Ku Klux Klan. Dunning was also clear who were the villains: vindictive radical Republicans; white Southern renegades (or 'scalawags'); and Northern 'carpetbaggers' who headed South to make a fast buck.

However, since about 1950 reconstruction has been viewed very differently. In the 1950s and 1960s, historians such as Kenneth Stampp and John Hope Franklin depicted reconstruction as an extraordinary lenient process. 'Rarely in history,' wrote Stampp, 'have participants in an unsuccessful rebellion endured so mild penalties as those Congress imposed upon the people of the South and particularly upon their leaders.' In Stampp and Franklin's opinion the reconstruction villains were President Johnson, white Southerners, and the Ku Klux Klan. The heroes were the radical Republicans and black freedmen who fought nobly (but ultimately unsuccessfully) for their rights. In this view, the freedmen, not white Southerners, were the real losers of reconstruction. Although they received freedom, Southern blacks remained second-class citizens.

More recently, however, scholars have tended to view reconstruction in a more positive light. Historians such as Richard Ransom and Eric Foner have stressed that blacks were major participants, not just passive victims, in the reconstruction process. Foner has argued that black participation in Southern political life after 1867 was a radical development: 'a massive experiment in interracial democracy without precedent in the history of this or any other country that abolished slavery in the nineteenth century'. Ransom has argued persuasively that blacks did much better economically after 1865 than used to be thought.

This chapter will examine the process of reconstruction down to 1868. The next chapter will consider whether it succeeded or failed.

2 Reconstruction During the War

From 1861, as Union troops pushed remorselessly into the Con-federacy, Lincoln's administration faced the problem of how to restore loyal governments in the rebel states. In fact, there was a series of inter-related problems. On what terms should the defeated states be reunited with the Union? How should 'rebel' Southerners be treated? Which - if any - should be excluded from power? What should happen to the ex-slaves? And who should decide reconstruction policy: Congress or the President? Northern opinion was divided on all these matters. There were differences between Republicans and Democrats. There were also differences within the Republican Party, particularly between Lincoln and the radicals.

Lincoln was convinced that reconstruction was a presidential concern. Certainly the Constitution gave him the power of pardon: he was also Commander-in-Chief. But he realised that once the war ended, his powers would be considerably reduced. If he was to control reconstruction, he needed to establish firm principles during the war. Lincoln's strategic aim was totally consistent throughout the war: he wanted to restore the Union as quickly as possible. His usual policy was to install a military governor in those states which had been partially reconquered. The governors were expected to work with whatever popular support they could find. Lincoln hoped that military government would only last until enough loyal citizens could form a new state government.

Lincoln spelt out his reconstruction ideas in more detail in a Proclamation in December 1863. He offered pardon (with certain exceptions) to white Southerners who would take an oath to support 'the Constitution of the United States and the union of the States'. When 10 per cent of the 1860 electorate had taken this oath of allegiance, a new state government could be established. Provided the state then accepted the abolition of slavery, Lincoln promised to recognise its government. In the spring and summer of 1864, Tennessee, Louisiana and Arkansas used Lincoln's '10 per cent Plan' to set up new governments. No one, least of all Lincoln, believed that the 10 per cent Plan laid out a comprehensive blueprint for the post-war South. At this stage in the war, Lincoln's aim was to win Southern support for the Union, thus weakening the Confederacy. Other potentially divisive issues, such as black suffrage, could be left to the end of the war.

Not all members of the Republican Party agreed with Lincoln's actions. Within the party there were deep divisions. Conservatives held very different views to the radicals. Most - moderate - Republicans were somewhere in between the two extremes. But it was not a time of tightly organised, ideologically unified politics: in consequence, the lines of division were blurred and there were constant shifts. It is difficult, therefore, for historians to label Republicans as 'radicals', 'moderates' or 'conservatives'.

During the war, the radicals tended to be the most vocal opponents of Lincoln. Their leaders included Thaddeus Stevens, a club-footed, acid-tongued, Pennsylvanian industrialist; Charles Sumner, the abolitionist Senator from Massachusetts who had risen to national fame when he had been savagely beaten by a Southern congressmen in 1856; and Benjamin Wade, a rough, hot-tempered, politician from Ohio. These men, like all the radicals, are difficult to categorise. Attempts to show that radicals had a distinctive personality-type are not convincing. The aristocratic, self-righteous and inflexible Sumner, had little in common in personality or political style with Thaddeus Stevens, a master both of Congressional in-fighting and blunt speaking.

However, radicals do seem to have had some things in common. Many represented 'safe' New England seats - or seats where there were large numbers of New England migrants. Many had sat in Congress for a long time. This may have given them a sense of common purpose. It certainly enhanced their influence at a time when most Congressmen only sat for one term. Experience counted and radical leaders invariably found themselves on the key committees. The careers of most radicals had been shaped well before the Civil War by the slavery controversies. Most had good abolitionist credentials. Both Sumner and Stevens had long advocated the unpopular cause of black suffrage.

Although radicals did not work in close and constant harmony with one another and did not hold the same views on every issue, by 1864 most held similar views with regard to reconstruction. Virtually all were dissatisfied with Lincoln's proposals which were seen as too lenient: they wanted a much harsher settlement which would punish those responsible for the war. Most were also concerned about the plight of the freed slave and believed they should have the same basic civil rights, including the right to vote, as white Americans. Some, like Stevens, believed it was possible to kill two birds with the same stone: punish the 'rebels' by confiscating their land; and assist the freedmen by giving each black family part of the confiscated land.

It has been claimed that radical concern for black rights, particularly black suffrage, was triggered by shabby political motives rather than idealism. Certainly, radicals feared that once the Southern states were back within the Union, the Democrat Party (which won 45 per cent of the Northern vote in 1864) must inevitably triumph. There seemed two ways to prevent this: first, ensure that Southern blacks could vote (they would surely vote Republican); and secondly, disfranchise large numbers of ex-Confederates.

Historians once claimed that radicals, some of whom were industrialists, had economic, as well as political, motives. A Democrat government might well overturn Republican economic measures such as high tariffs and government subsidies, from which radicals personally benefited. However, most historians are now convinced that selfish economic interest was not the main motivator of the radicals. Indeed, on the major economic issues of the day there was no unified radical position. While most radicals were worried about the future political situation, this did not necessarily mean that they were not sincerely concerned about black rights. Most radicals would probably have found it hard to separate idealism and political pragmatism. Thaddeus Stevens was convinced that blacks should be entitled to vote and not ashamed to assert that such a policy would ensure the ascendancy of the Republicans.

Whatever their motivation, most radicals believed that the Southern states, by illegally seceding, had reverted to the condition of territories and should thus be subject to Congress's authority. Congress, not the President, should thus control the reconstruction process.

Dissatisfaction with Lincoln's 10 per cent Plan became apparent in 1864. Developments in Louisiana, much of which had been under military occupation since 1862, sparked particular concern. In April

1864 a Louisiana convention had drawn up a constitution under which slavery was prohibited. However, the convention with the backing of the military governor, General Nathanial Banks, refused to allow blacks, 47 per cent of Louisiana's population, the right to vote. (Banks was against granting black suffrage in principle but also thought it would damage his efforts to win white Louisiana support.) Well over 10 per cent of the 1860 Louisiana electorate voted in favour of the proposed constitution. Lincoln immediately recognised the new Louisiana government and treated the state as if it had been restored to the Union.

Radicals, who favoured black suffrage, bitterly criticised developments in Louisiana. They managed to convince Congress to reject Louisiana's reconstructed constitution and to refuse admission to its two Senators. Two radicals, Henry Davis and Benjamin Wade, then introduced a bill requiring not 10 per cent but 50 per cent of the people of the Confederate states to take an 'Ironclad oath' - an oath that they never voluntarily supported the rebellion - before the states could return into the Union. Moreover, anyone who had held political office during the Confederacy or had voluntarily borne arms against the United States was to be excluded from the political process. It was likely to be many years before most Confederate states could meet these conditions. But it should be noted that the Wade-Davis bill was not a fully-fledged radical measure: it did not, for example, guarantee blacks equal political rights. Its main purpose was to postpone reconstruction until the war was over when Congress would have more control.

The Wade-Davis bill passed both Houses of Congress, with the almost unanimous support of Congressional Republicans. However, Lincoln, after some hard thinking, decided to veto the bill. His public explanation was that he wanted to support the reconstructed governments in Arkansas and Louisiana and see both states re-enter the Union. His veto caused a short but bitter political storm. Wade and Davis went to the length of publishing their own statement, which was highly critical of Lincoln's 'rash and fatal act'. But with the 1864 presidential elections only weeks away, most Republicans rallied round Lincoln, including - ultimately - both Wade and Davis. Nevertheless Lincoln's hopes of formulating a definitive method, accepted by Congress, by which former Confederate states would be allowed back into the Union, had failed.

This was by no means the only reconstruction problem. During the war neither Lincoln, Congress, nor Union army officers had been able to draw up a coherent policy with regard to assisting the former slaves. Fearing that blacks and whites could not live peacefully together and that blacks would never be afforded equal opportunities in the South (or North), Lincoln had supported the idea of colonising ex-slaves in West Africa, the Caribbean or Central America. During the war, several attempts had been made to put colonisation schemes into effect. But the schemes quickly floundered, largely because most African Americans refused to participate. Most thought they had as much right to stay in the country of their birth as whites. (Only 1 per cent of African Americans in 1860 had been born abroad.) Some abolitionists suggested that it would make more sense to transport rebel slaveowners than ex-slaves!

As Union forces reconquered large parts of the South, Lincoln's administration faced the problem of what to do with tens of thousands of ex-slaves. Given that the Union government found itself in control of large tracts of land either abandoned by Southerners or confiscated from them for non-payment of taxes, one solution was to simply redistribute the land to ex-slaves. Theoretically, the 1862 Confiscation Act made possible the wholesale forfeiture of Confederate property. But this penalty could only be imposed after court proceedings in individual cases. Moreover, and at Lincoln's insistence, the loss of property was limited to the lifetime of the owner and did not affect his or her heirs. Lincoln, aware that many Northerners were opposed to a major redistribution of property and fearing that such action would undermine his efforts to win the support of Southern whites, had little enthusiasm for large scale confiscation and the Act remained largely unenforced.

Given no firm presidential or Congressional guidance, the situation in the reoccupied areas of the Confederacy was chaotic, varying from place to place and from time to time. Federal agents in the South, especially army officers, instituted their own - experimental - remedies. The most famous 'rehearsal for reconstruction' occurred on the Sea Islands off the coast of South Carolina. These were occupied by Union forces as early as November 1861. Northern managers were appointed to run the plantations abandoned by slaveowners. The 10,000 ex-slaves were given wages but also their own garden plots. In 1862-3 the government decided that the lands should be sold. 16,000 acres were sold at auction. 600 acres were bought by individual blacks: 2,000 were purchased by groups of freedmen who pooled their resources. The remaining 14,000 acres were bought by Northern entrepreneurs who hoped to make money from cotton. But this well-publicised (albeit small-scale) development was not typical. In most places, plantations remained in government hands and were administered by 'superintendents of negro affairs' or leased to Northern investors, whose main purpose was profit. Other plantations were still controlled by former slaveholders who were prepared to take an oath of allegiance to the Union.

In these circumstances, life for most freedmen (and women) did not change very much. They continued to work on the same plantations and were usually closely supervised by white managers. They were now paid wages but these were invariably low, most of the money earned being withheld to pay for food and clothing. Both Northerners and 'loyal' Southern planters insisted that black labourers were forbidden to leave the plantations on which they worked without their employers' permission. But at least freedmen were no longer whipped and some new (and old) landowners increased incentives for those ex-slaves who worked hard. This system, sometimes seen as a half-way house between slavery and free labour, satisfied no one.

In January 1865 a (seemingly) great experiment was launched when General Sherman declared that coastal territory from Charleston to Florida, stretching 30 miles inland, should be set aside for freed slaves, with each black family to receive 40 acres and a surplus army mule. Sherman was far from a humanitarian reformer: his main concern was to relieve the pressure caused by the large number of impoverished blacks following his army. He also stipulated that Congress would have to reach a final decision on his plan. Nevertheless, some 40,000 blacks were given small farms. Elsewhere ex-slaves sometimes simply helped themselves to abandoned or confiscated land.

While Sherman's actions raised black hopes and expectations, federal policy toward black economic reconstruction remained uncertain and contradictory. Some Republicans were opposed to giving blacks any land - or help - whatsoever, arguing that property was sacrosanct and that blacks must learn to stand on their own feet. 'Are they free men or not?', asked Senator Grimes of Iowa in 1864. 'If they are free men, why not let them stand as free men?' However, by 1865 most Republicans in Congress seem to have favoured confiscating plantation land and redistributing it among the freedmen and 'loyal' whites. Such action would reward the deserving and punish the guilty. But Congressmen were unable to agree on a precise measure and thus failed to pass a redistribution bill.

In March 1865 Congress did agree to set up the Bureau of Refugees, Freedmen and Abandoned Lands (better known as the Freedmen Bureau). The aim of the Bureau was to help relieve the suffering of Southern blacks (and poor whites) by providing food, clothes, fuel and medical care. But the Bureau was also authorised to divide abandoned and confiscated land into 40 acre plots for redistribution to freedmen and 'loyal' white refugees. The Bureau was envisaged as a temporary expedient. Nevertheless, its creation symbolised the widespread belief among many Republicans that the federal government should shoulder some responsibility for the economic well-being of the freedmen.

While some Northerners were anxious to help the ex-slaves, few believed that blacks were equal to whites. Indeed many Northerners still had a real antipathy to blacks and feared an exodus of Southern blacks to the North. Racial tension was particularly strong in the four slave states which had remained within the Union. Most border-state whites had no wish to give blacks equal rights. (Kentucky still had 65,000 blacks in bondage in April 1865. Its legislature opposed the 13th Amendment to the bitter end and slavery survived in the state until December 1865.) During the war, a number of Northern states and cities had eliminated some of their discriminatory 'black laws'. But there was still only limited support for black suffrage: in 1865 only five Northern states allowed blacks to vote on equal terms with whites.

3 Lincoln's Position in 1865

Precisely where Lincoln stood on many reconstruction issues by the spring of 1865 is a matter of some debate. He certainly hoped to retain control of the process. On such matters as confiscation of property and punishment of Confederate leaders, he was prepared to be generous. In his second inaugural speech in March 1865, he said:

1 With malice towards none, with charity for all, with firmness in the right as God gives us to see the right, let us strive on to finish the work we are in, to bind up the nation's wounds, to care for him who shall have borne the battle and for his widow and his orphan,
5 to do all which may achieve and cherish a just and lasting peace among ourselves and with all nations.

But despite both his executive power and his political dexterity, Lincoln had failed to bring a single reconstructed state back into the Union. The Unionist governments, created in Tennessee, Arkansas and Louisiana, had not attracted much Southern support and had not been recognised by Congress. It was clear that Lincoln faced problems. His party, even his own cabinet, was divided on a host of reconstruction matters. Lincoln, himself, seems to have been moving cautiously towards supporting the view that black Americans should have equality before the law and by the spring of 1865 talked in terms of giving some black Americans - the 'very intelligent' and those who fought for the Union - the vote.

Reconstruction was discussed at Lincoln's last cabinet meeting on 14 April 1865. Those present disagreed on what Lincoln's views were: different men heard Lincoln say what they wanted him to say. What Lincoln would have done will remain forever a mystery for later that evening he was assassinated by John Wilkes Booth in the Ford Theatre in Washington. Booth escaped but within days had been tracked down and shot dead by federal troops. Four others - three men and a woman - who were supposedly involved in the 'conspiracy' were tried, found guilty and hung with unseemly but natural haste.

Most Northerners assumed that Confederate leaders had instigated the assassination. Some historians still claim there was a major conspiracy. But it seems far more likely that the assassination plot arose in the fevered mind of Booth alone. A supporter of the South, he had long wanted to strike a blow for the Confederate cause. The murder of Lincoln, however, did little to help that cause. Lincoln had been the South's best chance for a mild peace. His murder served only to harden the Northern mood.

4 Andrew Johnson

Vice President Andrew Johnson now became President. Ironically before the war Johnson had been a Democrat. Even more ironically, he was a Southerner and ex-slaveowner (from Tennessee). A self-made man who had risen from tailor's apprentice to prosperous landowner, he had considerable political experience, having held office almost continuously since 1829. In 1861 he had been the only Confederate state Senator to stay loyal to the Union. Lincoln had appointed him provisional governor of Tennessee. Then, in 1864, in an effort to balance the Republican/Unionist ticket, Johnson was nominated Vice President. Few envisaged he would ever become President. After his behaviour at Lincoln's inauguration in March 1865, few hoped he would become so. Recovering from illness, he had fortified himself with several tots of whisky to calm his nerves. Unfortunately the alcohol had more effect on his weakened condition than he had anticipated, resulting in his being - obviously - drunk. This lapse did considerable damage to his reputation.

Nevertheless, in 1865 a number of radical Republicans were (privately) pleased that Johnson had replaced Lincoln, even if they disliked the circumstances. Johnson had shown great courage during the war and total devotion to the Union. It seemed likely he would take a tough stand against the Confederate leaders, especially the great plantation owners, whom he had attacked throughout his political career. 'Traitors,' said Johnson in 1864, 'must be punished and impoverished.' This was the kind of talk that radicals liked to hear. 'We have faith in you,' Ben Wade told Johnson. 'By the Gods there will be no trouble now in running the government.'

Another radical, G.W. Julian of Indiana, referring to the day of Lincoln's death, wrote:

> 1 I spent most of the afternoon in a political caucus, held for the
> purpose of considering the necessity for a new Cabinet and a line of
> policy less conciliatory than that of Mr Lincoln: and while
> everybody was shocked at his murder, the feeling was nearly
> 5 universal that the accession of Johnson to the Presidency would
> prove a godsend to the country. Aside from Mr. Lincoln's known
> policy of tenderness to the Rebels ... his ... views of the subject of
> reconstruction were as distasteful as possible to Radical Republicans.

However, the Johnson-radical honeymoon was short-lived. Differences over reconstruction policies were soon to lead to bitter separation. Julian, for example, was soon describing Johnson as a 'genius in depravity ... devil-bent upon the ruin of his country'.

Historians, siding with the radicals, have generally given Johnson a poor press. He has been criticised for sharing the racial views of most white Southerners (and most Northern Democrats) and being unconcerned about the plight of ex-slaves. He has also been criticised for showing little political skill and for stubbornly ignoring the political mood in the North. However, some recent biographers have been more sympathetic to Johnson, arguing that his reconstruction policies were essentially right, his main failing being his inability to carry them out.

The situation facing Johnson in the South might have been worse. By May 1865 the war was effectively over. Although guerrilla war spluttered on in a few areas, most Confederate soldiers returned to their homes. This meant that Johnson's government could quickly demobilise Union armed forces. By December 1865 the Union army had shrunk to 150,000 men: by the end of 1866 it was only 38,000 strong.

However, Johnson did face difficult situations, both in the North and in the South, which would have tested the political skill of Lincoln. Southern problems were the most obvious. A quarter of all white Southern men of military age had died in the war. Large numbers had been wounded and maimed. (Mississippi spent 20 per cent of its revenue in 1865 on purchasing artificial limbs for Confederate veterans!) The Southern economy was in tatters. Union armies had caused widespread devastation, destroying cities, railroad lines, farm buildings and machinery, and killing or taking animals. The emancipation of the slaves meant that, at a stroke, the South had lost over $2 billion of capital. The Southern banking system was shattered and there was very little money in circulation. Large numbers of black and white Southerners were dependent for subsistence on federal aid.

The end of slavery meant the end of a whole way of life. Developing new social relations between blacks and whites was unlikely to be easy. Most blacks were delighted with freedom and relished the opportunity to flaunt their liberty and enjoy its material benefits. Many walked off the plantations to test their freedom, to search for loved ones who had been sold, or to seek their fortunes, particularly in the cities of the South. Most blacks wanted independence from white control. But many also demanded equal citizenship with whites. In the summer of 1865 black leaders organised a seemingly endless series of mass meetings and petitions demanding civil equality, particularly the right to vote. Demands for equal treatment were supported by scores of thousands of blacks who had served in the Union army. Military service had been a politicizing and radicalising experience for many Southern blacks, resulting in enhanced self-confidence. Ex-soldiers, often now literate thanks to army schools, frequently became the leaders of black political movements post 1865.

The fact that many blacks had great expectations (which it might be difficult to realise) was one problem. The attitude of Southern whites was another. The vast majority of Southern whites, rich and poor alike, did not consider blacks to be their equals. They were resentful and fearful of emancipated slaves. Many were appalled at what they saw as black insolence and insubordination and a wave of (mainly) white violence raged almost unchecked in many parts of the South. Blacks were often assaulted and sometimes murdered for trying to leave plantations or for not working. White Southerners were bitterly united by their defeat. Loathing of Northerners was widespread and, in some quarters, unrelenting. An innkeeper from North Carolina told one Northern journalist, the Yankees had killed his sons, burned his house and stolen his slaves: 'I git up at half-past four in the morning, and sit up till twelve at night, to hate 'em'. Most Southerners hated the Republican Party.

Johnson, who kept Lincoln's cabinet, claimed his intention was to continue Lincoln's reconstruction policy. Viewing reconstruction as an executive not a legislative function, he hoped to restore the Southern states to the Union before Congress met in December 1865. Anxious that the USA should return to its normal functioning as soon as possible and having no wish to continue an expensive military occupation of the South, Johnson saw no alternative but to work with ex-Confederates. In consequence he favoured adopting lenient policies which would win white Southern support. He was also totally committed to state rights, believing it was not the federal government's responsibility to decide suffrage issues or to involve itself in economic and social matters. Nor had he any wish to promote the position of ex-slaves. Shaped by a lifetime in Tennessee, he did not consider blacks to be equal to whites. He was particularly opposed to black suffrage which he thought would result in 'a tyranny such as this Continent has never yet witnessed'.

The main thrust of Johnson's intentions were soon apparent. In May 1865 he extended recognition to the Southern governments created under Lincoln's administration, none of which had enfranchised blacks. The same month he issued a general amnesty to most Southerners who were prepared to swear an oath of allegiance and support emancipation. Although major Confederate office holders and large landowners were exempted from the general pardon, they were allowed to apply individually for a special presidential pardon. Over the summer of 1865 much of Johnson's time was occupied in granting thousands of these pardons. Johnson also ordered that confiscated land be returned to pardoned Southerners. This necessitated the army evicting thousands of freedmen throughout the South.

Why Johnson so quickly abandoned the idea of punishing ex-Confederates and the Southern elite is something of a mystery. There were rumours at the time that some Southerners used bribery to win pardons. Others suspected that flattery by Southern planters and their wives played upon the President's ego. More likely, Johnson simply came to view co-operation with the Southern elite as indispensable to two inter-related goals: the maintenance of white supremacy in the South; and his own re-election as President in 1868. To achieve the latter, he needed to retain the support of Northern Republicans, win over moderate Northern Democrats and build up a following in the South.

Johnson made the process by which Southern states would return to the Union easy. He appointed provisional state governors who did their best to co-operate with white Southerners. Their main job was to hold elections for state conventions, chosen by the 'loyal' people of each state. (The franchise was still limited to whites!) The conventions then had the task of drawing up new constitutions which repealed the ordinances of secession and accepted that slavery was illegal. Once this was done the states would be readmitted to the Union.

Johnson's reconstruction scheme was approved by his cabinet and seemed (in 1865) to have the support of most Northerners. While many Republicans favoured black suffrage, few, apart from the radicals, saw it as a reason to repudiate the President. Moderate Republicans were anxious to keep their party united: they realised that black rights was a potentially divisive, and far from popular issue in the North.

5 'Reconstruction Confederate Style'

White Southerners, appreciating they had been given the freedom to shape their future, immediately set about implementing Johnson's terms. State conventions repudiated secession and acknowledged (albeit reluctantly) the end of slavery. The South then proceeded to elect legislatures, governors and members of Congress. In most Southern states men who had opposed secession in 1861 were swept into power. But very few of these men had actively opposed the Confederacy: indeed many had held high military or civilian office within it. The new Southern state governments immediately searched for legal means of keeping the freedmen under control. No state enfranchised blacks. All, by large majorities, introduced 'black codes'. These varied from state to state but all were designed to ensure that blacks were treated as second-class citizens. Most states required blacks to possess labour contracts which provided written evidence of employment. These contracts were designed to keep black wages low. Those blacks who were unemployed or who broke the contracts could be forcibly set to work. Black 'vagrants' - the idle, disorderly and those who lacked 'visible means of support' - could be punished by involuntary plantation labour. Black children could be taken as 'apprentices' and forcibly put to work on plantations. The codes ensured that blacks were not allowed to buy or rent land, marry whites or serve on juries. They were also usually barred from poor relief, orphanages and schools. The 'black codes' were enforced by a white judicial system that made little pretence of meting out justice fairly. Texas courts, for example, indicted some 500 white men for the murder of blacks in 1865-6: not one was convicted.

The aim of 'reconstruction Confederate style' was to resurrect as near as possible the old order. White Southerners, given their basic attitudes and assumptions, could hardly have been expected to act otherwise. President Johnson did not approve of all the developments in the South. In his December message to Congress he expressed some concern for the freedmen. But given his state rights' ideology, he believed he had no alternative but to accept what had occurred. He announced that the work of reconstruction - he termed it 'restoration' - was now complete. It has been suggested that had Johnson been firmer with the South in 1865, the defeated and demoralised white Southerners would have accepted whatever 'punishment' had been meted out and that this would somehow have changed the future for the better. Given white Southern prejudices, this seems highly unlikely.

6 Radical Republican Opposition

Most Northerners had been prepared to let Johnson try his lenient policy. But by the time Congress met in December 1865, there were many misgivings. After four years of war, Northerners still had a profound distrust of the South. The fact that the Southern Congressmen who turned up in Washington in December 1865 included Stephens (the Confederate Vice President), four Confederate generals and 58 members of the Confederate Congress, did not reassure Northerners of the South's good intent. Nor did the 'black codes'. It seemed to many that the war had been fought for no purpose. Unless the federal government took action blacks would not have equal opportunity. To make matters worse, there seemed every likelihood that Southern whites with their Northern Democrat allies would soon dominate the political scene. In 1865 Northern Democrats held only a quarter of the seats in Congress. The return of the Southern states would bring in 22 Senators and 63 members of the House of Representatives, the majority of whom would presumably be Democrat.

Republicans, who identified the interests of their party with those of the nation, were determined not to be tricked out of the fruits of victory. Most Republican Congressmen were moderates, not radicals. But moderates, like radicals, felt that Southerners should change their ways before being readmitted to the Union. Virtually all Republicans believed that Confederate leaders should be prevented from holding office and that the basic rights of ex-slaves should be protected.

But moderate Republicans were in something of a dilemma. They had no wish to bring about social revolution in the South. Nor did they wish to break with Johnson. Many of them were not enthusiastic about the prospect of black suffrage, which they knew to be a political liability in the North, and which seemed less likely to provide a stable basis for a Southern Republican Party than a political alliance with forward-looking white Southerners. Nor had most moderate Republicans any desire greatly to expand federal authority. Yet most of the rights they sought to guarantee for blacks had always been state concerns.

The Republican-dominated Congress had no difficulty agreeing not to admit the Southern Congressmen. It also refused to recognise the new regimes in the South. In an effort to control future developments, a joint Committee on Reconstruction was set up to make recommendations for a new policy. This Committee had the support of most Republicans and was not dominated by radicals. The moderate Republican majority still hoped to work out a compromise that would guarantee basic rights to Southern blacks and be acceptable to Johnson.

Johnson now made a major political blunder. Instead of working with the moderate Republicans, he chose to nail his colours to the Southern - or at least Democrat - mast. When Congress tried to enlarge the powers of the Freedmen Bureau, Johnson vetoed it, claiming that it was an unwarranted continuation of war power. Moderate Republicans were horrified. Despite facing a Herculanean task, the Bureau had operated quite effectively, providing basic welfare provision for ex-slaves. Johnson's veto helped convince many Republicans that they could no longer work with the President. The Democrats, by contrast, were delighted by Johnson's veto and held a number of mass meetings in Washington to endorse his stand. Johnson actually addressed one such mass rally, comparing the radical Republicans to Judas Iscariot and likening himself to Christ.

Moderate and radical Republicans now brought forward a Civil Rights Bill which aimed to guarantee minimal rights to blacks in the South. Defining all people born in the United States (except untaxed Indians) as national citizens, the measure asserted the right of the federal government to intervene in state affairs where and when necessary to protect the rights of US citizens. Moderates still hoped that Johnson would accept this measure and the Bill received the virtual unanimous support of the Congressional Republicans. Despite pressure from his cabinet, Johnson stuck to his guns. Arguing that civil rights were a state matter, he vetoed the measure. Congress now struck back. In April 1866 a two-thirds majority ensured that Johnson's veto was over-ridden and the Civil Rights Bill became law. A few weeks later Congress passed a second version of the Freedmen Bureau bill. When Johnson vetoed it, his veto was again overridden with all but three Republicans in the Senate voting against the President.

Then, to ensure that civil rights could not be changed in future, Congress set about adopting the 14th Amendment which embodied the Civil Rights Act. As well as providing a definition of American citizenship, it went on to guarantee all citizens equality before the law. If individual states tried to abridge the rights of American citizens, the federal government could intervene. The Amendment also banned from office Confederates who before the war had taken an oath of allegiance to the Union, required of officials ranging from the President down to postmasters. This made virtually the entire political leadership of the

South ineligible for office. This was quite specific. But much of the 14th Amendment was simply a broad statement of principle and was thus open to differing interpretations. The following is the important Section 1:

1 All persons born or naturalized in the United States, and subject to the jurisdiction thereof, are citizens of the United States and of the State wherein they reside. No State shall make or enforce any law which shall abridge the privileges or immunities of citizens of the
5 United States; nor shall any State deprive any person of life, liberty, or property, without due process of law; nor deny to any person within its jurisdiction the equal protection of the laws.

Some radicals interpreted this literally: they assumed that henceforward all men (except Indians) were equal. Most moderates, on the other hand, did not imagine that after the Amendment was ratified, blacks would become fully equal with whites, voting in elections, sitting on juries and attending mixed schools. The fact that the 14th Amendment could be interpreted differently ensured that it was quickly adopted by both Houses of Congress and then passed to the states for approval. Johnson could do nothing except protest. Not surprisingly the Amendment was rejected by all the ex-Confederate states (except Tennessee), and also by Delaware and Kentucky. It therefore failed to gain the approval of the 75 per cent of states that was necessary for it to become law.

That summer there were serious race riots in the South, first in Memphis (in May) and then in New Orleans (in July). Gangs of Southern whites, often supported by the police, attacked black 'agitators', resulting in some 80 to 90 black deaths. The riots received wide publicity in the North. Most Northerners were appalled. They were similarly appalled by the rise of secret quasi-military organisations, like the Knights of the White Camelia, the Sons of Midnight and the Ku Klux Klan, which aimed to terrorise blacks and those Southern whites who sympathised with blacks.

By June 1866 Johnson had few supporters in the Republican Party. But he was not prepared passively to accept the defeat of his own reconstruction programme. The 1866 mid-term elections seemed to provide him with an opportunity to strengthen his position. Hoping to unite Democrats and conservative Republicans, he supported the gathering of the National Union Convention which met in Philadelphia in July. The Convention called for the election of Congressmen who would support Johnson's policies. Johnson threw himself vigorously into the election campaign, speaking in many of America's largest cities. This unprecedented effort backfired. Confronted by hecklers, Johnson often lost his temper and in so doing surrendered his presidential dignity. Moreover, his hopes of establishing a new party did not materialise. The

National Union movement soon became little more than the Democrat Party in a new guise. The Republican Party had no difficulty campaigning against both Johnson and the Democrats. Republican propaganda depicted Johnson as a drunkard, a rake, and a man touched with insanity. Republican leaders harked back to the war, insisting that the fruits of victory would be lost if Northerners voted Democrat/ National Union.

The election results were a disaster for Johnson and a triumph for the Republican Party which won every state, except Delaware, Maryland and Kentucky. In the new Congress, Johnson's Republican opponents would have a comfortable two-thirds majority in both Houses of Congress, thus ensuring they could over-ride any presidential veto.

7 Radical - or Congressional - Reconstruction

The 39th, Republican-dominated, Congress which met between December 1866 and March 1867 now took over the reconstruction process.

Thaddeus Stevens set out his terms in January 1867:

1 Unless the rebel States, before admission, should be made republican in spirit, and placed under the guardianship of loyal men, all our blood and treasure will have been spent in vain. I waive now the question of punishment which, if we are wise, will
5 still be inflicted by moderate confiscations, both as a reproof and example. Having these States ... entirely within the power of Congress, it is our duty to take care that no injustice shall remain in their organic laws...
   There is more reason why coloured voters should be admitted in
10 the rebel States than in the Territories. In the States they form the great mass of the loyal men. Possibly with their aid loyal governments may be established in most of those States. Without it all are sure to be ruled by traitors; and loyal men, black and white, will be oppressed, exiled or murdered... Have not loyal blacks quite
15 as good a right to choose rulers and make laws as rebel whites? ... The white Union men are in a great minority in each of those States. With them the blacks would act in a body; and it is believed that in each of the said States, except one, the two united would form a majority, control the States, and protect themselves ...
20 Another good reason is, it would insure the ascendency of the Union party. Do you avow the party purpose? exclaims some horror-stricken demagogue. I do. For I believe, on my conscience, that on the continued ascendency of that party depends the safety of this great nation. If impartial suffrage is excluded in rebel States
25 then every one of them is sure to send a solid rebel representative

delegation to Congress, and cast a solid rebel electoral vote. They, with their kindred Copperheads in the North, would always elect the President and control Congress... For these among other reasons, I am for negro suffrage in every rebel State. If it be just, it 30 should not be denied; if it be necessary, it should be adopted; if it be a punishment to traitors, they deserve it.

Stevens did not speak for all Republicans. Given that Congress was by no means dominated by the radicals, Johnson might still have had some room for manouevre had he been prepared to compromise. But it was soon clear that he had no intention of trying to do so.

In the spring of 1867 Congress passed a far-reaching Military Reconstruction Bill. This stated that no legal government as yet existed in any Southern state, with the exception of Tennessee. No member from any ex-Confederate state was to be admitted into either the Senate or the House until Congress had declared that such states were entitled to representation. In the meantime the ten unreconstructed states were divided into five military districts, each placed under a federal commander whose military powers were superior to those of the existing state governments (which the Bill did not immediately replace). To get back into the Union, the Southern states had to elect constitutional conventions which would accept black suffrage, ratify the 14th Amendment and disqualify Confederate officeholders from participating in the democratic process. The new constitution had then to be ratified by a majority of the qualified voters.

The Bill did not create new federal agencies committed to protecting black rights. It made no economic provision for the freedmen. Nor did it massively disenfranchise Southern whites: this was seen as a state matter. But even so, the Bill appalled most Southern whites. It also appalled Johnson who claimed it would 'Africanize' half the country. He vetoed the Bill but it passed over his veto and thus became law.

Congress then moved to reduce Johnson's power. A Command of the Army Act, recognising the importance of the army in the reconstruction process, stated that all orders to subordinate army commanders were to pass through General Grant. Besieged by radicals on one hand and Johnson's friends on the other, Grant (easily the most popular man in the North) had tried to be non-committal, but by 1867 was fast drifting into the anti-Johnson camp.

Congress also passed the Tenure of Office Act. This was intended primarily to protect lower level patronage functionaries from being dismissed by Johnson. But the Act also barred the removal, without Senate approval, of any cabinet member during the term of the President who appointed them. This was designed to protect Secretary of War Stanton, a fierce critic of the President, who had still not resigned from his cabinet. Johnson did not accept this muzzling without a fight and plotted to dismiss Stanton (who had actually been appointed by

Lincoln!). In August 1867 when the Senate had adjourned for the summer, he suspended Stanton and persuaded General Grant to take over the War Office until the Senate reconvened. To further impede his Republican opponents, Johnson removed the military district officers who were vigorously enforcing the Reconstruction Acts, replacing them with men who were more sympathetic to the South.

State election results in the autumn of 1867 indicated that many Northerners shared some of Johnson's views, especially his opposition to black equality. Democrats, who played on Northern racial fears, made significant gains. The President regarded this as a vindication of his stand. But as soon as Congress reconvened in January 1868, he was again in trouble. The Senate refused to endorse the suspension of Stanton. Grant decided to move out of the office of Secretary of War and Stanton moved back into his old job. Johnson accused Grant of disloyalty and the two men exchanged angry letters, which found their way into the newspapers. The President now took the rash step of dismissing Stanton outright in defiance of the spirit (if not the actual wording) of the Tenure of Office Act. The immediate result was comical. Stanton refused to surrender his position and barricaded himself in his office. But far more important was the fact that Republicans in the House of Representatives, convinced that Johnson had broken the law, determined in February 1868 (by 126 votes to 47) to impeach him for 'high crimes and misdemeanours in office'. The House then appointed a committee to report the articles of impeachment. In so doing, the House ignored constitutional impeachment procedures, which called for an investigation first and then, if warranted, drawing up formal charges. Johnson, in effect, was presumed guilty before he was tried.

The impeachment proceedings took place in the Senate in the spring of 1868. Johnson faced a mixed bag of charges but essentially they narrowed down to the removal of Stanton from office, assertion of authority over the army, and non-co-operation with Congress. Underpinning these 'crimes' was the fact that many Republicans were out for revenge and/or anxious to get rid of Johnson who they believed was impeding the implementation of Congress's reconstruction policy. After a two month trial, 35 Senators finally voted against Johnson and only 19 (7 Republicans and 12 Democrats) for him. But the Constitution laid down that a two-thirds majority was necessary to impeach the President. Accordingly Johnson escaped by one vote. Although he had survived, for the rest of his term he was very much a 'lame duck' President. Nevertheless he still did all he could to water down Congress's actions. By December 1868, for example, he had given pardons to almost every leading Southerner.

8 President Grant

In 1868 the Republican Party rallied round General Grant, unanimously nominated on the first ballot at the Republican convention in Chicago. Grant had shown relatively little interest in party politics and had voted Democrat before the Civil War. However, he was ambitious, felt honoured to be nominated and thought it was his duty to stand. Without ever being a fully-fledged radical, he was quite prepared to support Congressional reconstruction. His Democrat opponent was Horatio Seymour, wartime governor of New York. Seymour and the Democrats opposed Republican reconstruction and campaigned against black equality. Although Grant won the election and gained a comfortable majority in the electoral college by 214 votes to 80, he won only 52 per cent of the popular vote - 3,012,000 votes to Seymour's 2,703,000 votes. Most Southern blacks supported Grant. The majority of white Americans, therefore, almost certainly voted for Seymour.

Given the election result, the Republican Party had even better cause to support black suffrage. In 1869 a new Amendment - the 15th - was introduced. This stated that, 'The right to vote should not be denied ... on account of race, colour or previous conditions of servitude'. To Democrats, this seemed a revolutionary measure - the crowning act of a Republican plot to promote black equality. Although some feminists were critical of the Amendment because it said nothing about giving women the vote, most Northern reformers hailed the Amendment as the triumphant conclusion to the decades of struggle on behalf of black Americans. A few years earlier such an Amendment would have been inconceivable. As late as 1868 only eight Northern states allowed blacks to vote. However, the Amendment did not explicitly guarantee all male citizens the right to vote. It did not forbid states to introduce literacy, property and educational tests which, while apparently non-racial, might effectively prevent the majority of blacks from voting.

The 15th Amendment was finally ratified in 1870. That same year the American Anti-Slavery Society disbanded, its leaders claiming that its work was complete and that blacks had received all the help they needed. With civil and political equality apparently assured, most Republicans believed that blacks no longer possessed a claim upon the federal government. Their status in society would now depend upon themselves. While committed to what had been accomplished, Northerners felt there was not much need to intervene more in Southern state affairs. Henceforward, the central political battleground of reconstruction would shift from Washington to the South.

Making notes on '*The Problem of Reconstruction, 1865-8*'

Your notes on this chapter should give you an overview of some of the main historiographical debates about reconstruction. More importantly, however, your notes should give you an understanding of the exact process of reconstruction down to 1868. As you read the chapter try to identify the main problems underlying that process. Also try to identify what action the Northern political establishment might have taken that was different. Should the North have taken stronger action against the Confederate states sooner? Could Lincoln have done more than he did before his assassination? Did Johnson continue Lincoln's policies? Should Johnson be blamed or praised for his efforts at reconstruction? How might white Southern attitudes have been changed? Given white attitudes, was more achieved for Southern blacks than might have been anticipated in 1865? The last batch of questions are ones to keep in mind as you read the next chapter.

Source-based questions on '*The Problem of Reconstruction, 1865-8*'

1 Lincoln's position in 1865
Read the short extract from Lincoln's second inaugural speech on page 27 and Julian's comment on the situation in April 1865 on page 28. Answer the following questions:
a) To what extent do Lincoln's words support Julian's opinions of the President's intentions? (4 marks)
b) Why might Lincoln's view of the situation in March 1865 have been different from his view of the situation in April 1865? (3 marks)
c) What were a group of radical Republicans plotting to do on the day of Lincoln's assassination - and why? (3 marks)
d) How might historians try to work out what most Northerners felt about reconstruction? (5 marks)

2 Thaddeus Stevens and Reconstruction
Read Stevens' speech to Congress in January 1867 on pages 35-6. Answer the following questions:
a) Was Stevens a typical Republican? Explain your answer. (4 marks)
b) To what extent was Stevens in favour of punishing the South? (4 marks)
c) What were Stevens' main arguments in support of black suffrage? (4 marks)
d) Comment on the phrase: 'It is our duty to take care that no injustice shall remain in their organic laws'. (4 marks)
e) What did Stevens mean when he talked of 'kindred Copperheads in the North'? (4 marks)

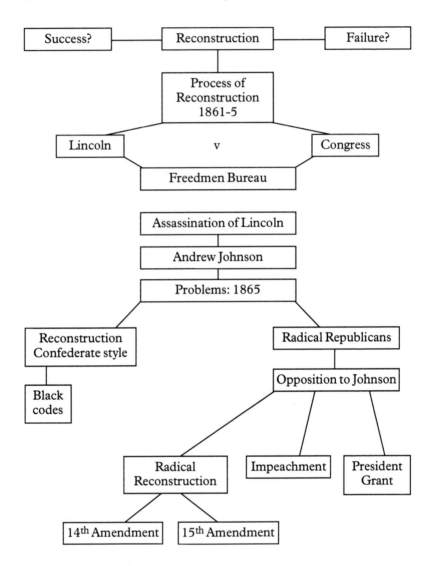

Summary - The Problem of Reconstruction, 1865-8

CHAPTER 3

Reconstruction in the South

1 Introduction

Following the Military Reconstruction Act, all the former Confederate states, except Tennessee, were to be under military rule before being eventually readmitted to the Union. The extent to which the South was under the heel of a 'military despotism' should not be exaggerated. By 1871 all the states had been readmitted to the Union and at no time were there more than 20,000 troops in the whole of the South. The main purpose of the army units was to ensure that democratic processes - of sorts - prevailed and that blacks, in particular, were registered to vote. Anxious to maintain order and avoid bloodshed, some commanders banned parades and forbade Confederate veterans to form organised groups. Some of the military commanders, like Generals Sheridan and Sickles who tried to adhere to the letter of the law, were heartily disliked. But others, sympathising with the white Southerners and/or doubting their ability to maintain order even in the limited areas where their troops were concentrated, adopted a generally light-handed approach. A few became genuinely popular. General Rousseau, who replaced Sheridan in Louisiana, so endeared himself to Southern whites by his almost total inaction that, when he died unexpectedly, his funeral procession was one of the largest ever seen in New Orleans.

From the autumn of 1867 onwards Southern Republicans produced the necessary constitutions and (in every state except Virginia) took over the first restored state governments. Large numbers of white Southerners did not participate in the electoral process. Many were disqualified from office: some were barred from voting by individual states; and others simply ignored the proceedings. Across the South, Republicans won resounding victories for the constitutional conventions. The constitutions which emerged from the conventions were generally enlightened. They established universal male suffrage, removed property qualifications for voting and holding power, gave most Southern states their first system of universal public education, reformed local government, obligated states to care for the disadvantaged - the insane, orphans, the deaf and dumb - and reformed the legal system. White Southerners tried to prevent ratification of the new constitutions by intimidation and by boycotting the polls so that the required majority of registered voters could not be mustered in their favour. After this tactic worked in Alabama, Congress quickly eliminated the majority requirement. The result was that Alabama, Arkansas, Florida, Georgia, Louisiana, North Carolina and South Carolina quickly ratified their respective constitutions and went on to install Republican governments. After ratification of the 14th Amendment, they were received back into the Union in June 1868. In

Georgia, military rule was temporarily revived when the state legislature expelled its new black members. After re-seating them, Georgia was re-admitted to the Union in 1870 along with Texas, Virginia and Mississippi.

Legally reconstruction seemed to be complete. However, most white Southerners were not prepared to accept the new situation. 'These constitutions and governments,' declared a Democrat newspaper, 'will last just as long as the bayonets which ushered them into being shall keep them in existence and not one day longer.' Republican governments in the South frequently did depend on the support of federal troops. However, Southern Republicans in 1867-8 did have a reasonable, indeed often considerable, amount of popular support and thus some kind of democratic mandate to rule. This support came from three groups: the newly enfranchised blacks; 'carpetbaggers' - Northern whites who had ventured South; and 'scalawags' - Southern whites who opposed the Democrat Party. By 1868 the Southern Republican Party seemed in very good health for an organisation which had scarcely existed on Southern soil in 1867. But throughout the South, the Republicans faced fierce opposition from white Democrats who sought to 'redeem' their states.

2 Black Reconstruction

There is considerable debate about the effectiveness of radical reconstruction in the South. Professor Dunning in the early twentieth century often referred to the period of Southern Republican rule as 'Black Reconstruction'. In Dunning's view the new governments represented the worst elements in Southern society - illiterate blacks, self-seeking Northerners and renegade Southern whites - given power by

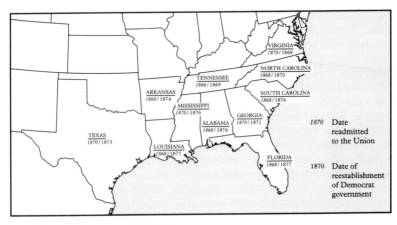

Southern states return to the Union

a vengeance-seeking Republican Congress. Dunning depicted 'Black Reconstruction' as essentially undemocratic, with the Republicans ruling against the will of a disfranchised white majority. He also accused the Republican governments of corruption on a grand scale.

However, most of Dunning's views have been challenged, including the very term 'Black Reconstruction' which implies that black Americans dominated the reconstruction process. This was at best a half-truth. Black Southerners certainly wielded some political power. Having been given the vote, most blacks were determined to use it and large numbers flocked to join the Union League, which became an important arm of the Republican Party in the South. To encourage black voters, the League organised secret lodges with elaborate initiation ceremonies and Masonic-like rituals. In two states - South Carolina and Mississippi - black voters constituted a 'real' majority of the electorate. In three other states (by September 1867) registered black voters outnumbered whites because so many 'rebels' were (temporarily) disenfranchised. The result was that in the two decades after 1867, Southern blacks were elected to national, state and local office. Two black Senators and 15 black Representatives were elected to Congress before 1877. About a quarter of the delegates to the constitutional conventions in 1867-8 were black. Many blacks were elected to state legislatures and for a time blacks actually controlled the lower house of South Carolina's legislature.

But while this was a revolutionary break with the past, black power and political influence, from the top of the political order to the bottom, never reflected black numbers. Very few of the top positions in state governments went to blacks. In five Southern states no black held a major office during reconstruction. The majority of black officeholders were local officials e.g. JPs and superintendents of education. But even at this level blacks did not hold a proportionate share of offices. Black leaders, especially in those states with large black populations, increasingly balked at the fact that they were merely junior partners in white-dominated Republican coalitions.

A number of reasons have been put forward to explain why black office-holders did not equate (relatively) with black voters. Some historians have stressed the lack of black experience, education, and organisation. Some have focused on black inertia and the habit of accepting white leadership. Others have argued that serious divisions within the black community, particularly between free-born blacks (who tended to see themselves as natural leaders of the black community) and ex-slaves (who often resented free black pretensions), weakened the black cause. There were also differences between black 'haves' (who were often free-born) and 'have-nots'. But perhaps the main reason why relatively few blacks were elected to office was the fact that blacks were a minority in most states. If they were to elect Republican governments, they needed to win white support. Assured of black support, come what may, the Republicans frequently put forward white candidates for office, hoping by so doing to attract more white voters. Moreover, many Republicans, North and South, privately shared the Democrat view that blacks were not competent to govern.

Most of the black leaders in the South were moderates who displayed little vindictiveness towards the white 'rebels'. Few showed much enthusiasm for disfranchising former Confederates and banning them from state politics. Nor did most display any great wish to support a policy of confiscation of plantation land and redistribution to freedmen. Some present-day historians have blamed (an essentially) black bourgeois leadership for betraying the black peasants who wanted land. However, it is unfair - and unhistorical - to blame black nineteenth-century leaders for failing to behave like twentieth-century socialists! Black leaders were aware that a radical land policy would probably have alienated white Southerners who Republicans were desperately seeking to attract.

3 Carpetbaggers and Scalawags

If the notion that reconstruction was imposed on the South by blacks is wrong, so also is the notion that it was controlled by Northern carpetbaggers who sought to profit at the South's expense. Relatively few Northerners ever actually settled in the South: in no state did they constitute even 2 per cent of the total population. Nor were all carpetbaggers set on fleecing the South economically. Many of the Northerners who went South were young, well-educated and middle-class. Some were teachers, clergy, officers of the Freedmen Bureau or agents of the various benevolent societies engaged in aiding the ex-slaves. Some were army veterans who had served in the South, liked what they saw and determined to remain there. Others were talented lawyers, businessmen and newspaper editors who headed South (often taking considerable capital with them) hoping for personal advancement. But most supported the Republican Party, not for selfish gain, but simply because they believed that Republican policies were best for both the country and for the South.

Without winning some support from Southern-born whites, the Republican governments would not have been elected. The 'scalawags' are difficult to categorise: they came from diverse backgrounds and voted Republican for a variety of reasons. Some were rich planters, merchants and industrialists who had once belonged to the Whig Party and who had always opposed the Democrats. Others were self-sufficient farmers, usually from upland areas, many of whom had opposed the Confederacy during the war. Some scalawags possessed considerable political experience. Governor Brown of Georgia, for example, for a time urged whites to vote Republican, thinking this was the best way to attract Northern capital needed for the development of Georgia.

Most scalawags, while prepared to guarantee black political and civil rights, did not support full racial equality. Like most Americans, they took racial separation for granted. The alliance with the blacks was a marriage of convenience. They realised that if they were to have any chance of maintaining political control, they must retain the black vote.

4 'A Saturnalia of Robbery and Jobbery'?

Southern Democrats bitterly attacked Republican - or radical - rule in the South. Their criticisms were echoed by 'neutral' contemporaries and (later) by historians. According to the English peer, Lord Bryce, the Republican governments in the South were responsible for, 'a Saturnalia of robbery and jobbery'. Historians have found plenty of evidence to collaborate this charge. Many Republican politicians were certainly corrupt. Bribery, especially by railroad companies, was commonplace. Ruling Republicans used their powers of patronage to benefit their own supporters. Nor is there any doubt that some Republican administrations were incompetent and inefficient. Southern state debts multiplied and taxes had to be sharply increased. The Freedmen Bureau has also come in for attack. It was charged at the time (and since) with being a corrupt and inefficient Republican tool and for encouraging a dependency culture.

However, most historians now view radical reconstruction in a different light. They point out that the late 1860s and 1870s saw corruption, bribery and inefficiency everywhere in the USA. Corruption in the South did not begin to compare with that in New York. Moreover, historians have shown that there was massive corruption in Southern state governments pre-1861 and also similar corruption after the Southern states had been 'redeemed'. The Republican governments in the South had actually little option but to raise and spend large sums of money. Most inherited empty treasuries and large public debts. Much of the Southern transportation system had been destroyed during the war. Public buildings needed to be repaired. Schools, orphanages and asylums had to be constructed as state governments accepted increased responsibility for a variety of welfare matters for black - as well as white - citizens. Interestingly, Democrat-controlled areas seem to have (over)spent just as much as Republican-controlled areas. The fact that new schools, hospitals, asylums, prisons and railroads were built across the South indicates that much of the money raised and spent by Republican governments was not wasted.

Historians have also come to the defence of the Freedmen Bureau. Although it lacked sufficient funds, it seems to have a good record in terms of providing blacks and poor whites with basic health-care, education and jobs. Bureau agents continued to monitor state and local judicial proceedings on behalf of blacks to try to ensure that justice was done. Most Bureau agents remained deeply committed to the idea of equality before the law.

The excesses of the reconstruction governments were invariably blamed on black members, even though power in Southern states remained largely in white control. In reality, those blacks who came to office performed as well - and as badly - as whites. Some were honest, intelligent and industrious: others were not. Most were professionals (clergymen predominated), artisans, independent farmers or small businessmen. A sizeable percentage were from the North and most were literate.

5 Economic Reconstruction

Southern Republicans liked to see themselves as belonging to the party of progress. They believed that state-sponsored capitalist development, particularly the encouragement of railroad building, would bring prosperity to their region. From 1867 to 1873 the South benefited from general American prosperity and from (short-lived) high cotton prices. Southern railroads were rebuilt and some 3,300 miles of new track were added. There was also an increase in textile - and other - manufacturing. But promising as this rehabilitation was, it did not keep pace with the industrial progress of the rest of the USA. The belief that railroad building would be the great panacea proved illusory. State investment in

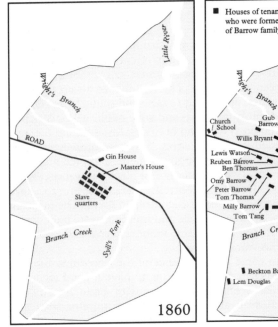
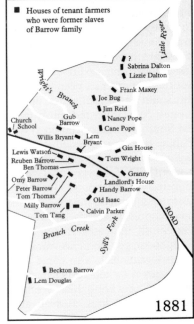

Changes on the Barrow Plantation, 1860-81

railroads simply led to ever-rising debts, higher taxes, and drained resources for schools and other projects.

Republican hopes of economic diversity, prosperity and modernisation failed to materialise. Short of cash and credit, the South remained an essentially agricultural region, heavily dependent on cotton. In many parts of the South the old plantations remained, sometimes with new owners, sometimes not. Blacks continued to do most of the hard labour. Some worked as labourers for very low wages. But during the 1870s most became sharecroppers. White landowners provided the land, seed, tools and direction, while black tenants supplied the labour. Whatever crop was produced was divided in a fixed ratio - often 50 per cent to the landowner and 50 per cent to the tenant. Although many planters resisted sharecropping, regarding it as inefficient and a threat to their authority, most had to accept it or lose their work force. Sharecropping - the most common but by no means the only form of land tenure - at least solved the labour shortage. It provided black farmers with freedom from day-to-day white supervision, a sense of ownership, and (in theory) some incentive to work hard.

But neither the independence nor the incentive should be exaggerated. Most of the sharecroppers' contracts were drawn up with a view to safeguarding the interests of the landlord. Then, in the early 1870s, a world-wide glut of cotton led to a disastrous fall in prices which resulted in most sharecroppers being in a perpetual state of indebtedness to both landowner and local storekeeper. In turn, landowners and storekeepers were often in debt to Southern merchants and bankers, who themselves were heavily in debt to Northern banks. These piled-up debts ensured that the South remained mainly a one-crop economy because everyone pressed the people below to produce crops that had a ready market value - chiefly cotton. The South did remarkably well in terms of total cotton output. In 1860 it had produced about 4.500,000 bales of cotton. By 1880, this figure had risen to over 6,350,000 bales. But the increased production simply added to the glut of cotton with the result that prices continued to tumble. And the only way for farmers to make ends meet was to try to produce more!

Despite the efforts of the Republicans, the South remained the poorest section in the United States. In 1860 the Southern states had controlled 30 per cent of the nation's wealth. In 1870 they controlled only 12 per cent. In 1860 the average white Southerner's income was similar to that of the average Northerner. By 1870 Southern income had dropped to less than two fifths of the Northern average. The radical governments were as much victims as perpetrators of this situation - a situation which continued long after the Southern states had been 'redeemed'. Nevertheless they can be criticised. Taxes, which tended to hit small landowners, might have been distributed more equitably. Too much reliance was placed on railroad building. Instead of bringing prosperity to the South, railroad construction tended to result in seedy corruption which tarnished the image of the Republican regimes. Those same regimes could certainly have done more to improve economic opportunities for blacks. Little was done to break up the great plantations and redistribute land, or even to share out the vast tracts of uncultivated land in the South. Few freedmen received the 40 acres and a mule which they had hoped to get in 1865.

6 White Resistance

The Republicans failed to win the support of most Southern whites who never regarded the radical governments as legitimate. Even had they been massively successful economically, it is unlikely they would have won great popularity. Most white Southerners harboured strong racist attitudes. The Republican reliance on black support meant the party was unlikely to attract mass white support. Republican rule, in fact, was to spark a vigorous backlash as Southern whites determined to recover political ascendancy.

Violence, mainly inflicted on blacks by whites, had been endemic in parts of the South since 1865. But radical reconstruction stimulated its growth. In 1866 paramilitary groups formed in most of the ex-Confederate states to fight for white rights. The most notorious of the groups was the Ku Klux Klan. The Klan, established in Tennessee and led for a time by the war hero General Nathan Bedford Forrest, spread rapidly in the years 1868-71. (Forrest set the number of Klansmen in Tennessee at 40,000 and in the South as a whole at over 500,000.)

According to the Klan's 'Organization and Principles' in 1868:

1 This is an institution of chivalry, humanity, mercy and patriotism; embodying in its genius and its principles all that is chivalric in conduct, noble in sentiment, generous in manhood, and patriotic in purpose; its peculiar objectives being: First, to protect the weak,
5 the innocent, and the defenseless from the indignities, wrongs, and outrages of the lawless, the violent, and the brutal; to relieve the injured and oppressed; to succor the suffering and unfortunate, and especially the widows and orphans of Confederate soldiers. Second, to protect and defend the Constitution of the United
10 States, and all laws passed in conformity thereto, and to protect the states and the people thereof from all invasion from any source whatever. Third, to aid and assist in the execution of all constitutional laws, and to protect the people from unlawful seizure and from trial, except by their peers in conformity to the
15 law of the land... The officers of this Order shall consist of a Grand Wizard of the Empire and his ten Genii; a Grand Dragon of the Realm and his eight Hydras; a Grand Titan of the Dominion and his six Furies; a Grand Giant of the Province and his four Goblins;

a Grand Cyclops of the Den and his two Night Hawks; a Grand
20 Magi, a Grand Monk, a Grand Scribe, a Grand Exchequer, a
Grand Turk, and a Grand Sentinel... The body politic of this
Order shall be known and designated as 'Ghouls'.

Despite its apparent Southern-wide organisation, the Klan operated
mainly at a local level, seeking to destroy Republican political
organisations by intimidation and terror. In the early twentieth century,
historians often claimed that the Klan arose for understandable reasons.
It was seen as a natural reaction to the rise of the Union Leagues and
radical tyranny. Indeed the Klan was lavished with praise and honour in
Thomas Dixon's novel *The Clansman* (subsequently adapted for the
cinema in D.W. Griffith's 1915 epic, 'The Birth of a Nation') for
helping deliver the South from the scourge of Black Republicans.

Historians in the second half of the twentieth century have been far
more critical of the Klan's terrorist activities, which reached their peak
in the years 1869-71. Blacks who held public office were particular
targets. So were black schools and churches. Recent research has shown
that the Klan was by no means simply an organisation of poor whites, as
some Democrat leaders implied. In fact it drew support from all sections
of the white community and was often encouraged in its violent actions
by 'respectable' Southern Democrat leaders.

In most Southern states Republican governments tried to prescribe
the Klan's activities by introducing laws which banned people from
joining organisations that disturbed the peace: some states even
outlawed the wearing of masks in public. But most states found it hard
to enforce the so-called 'Ku Klux Klan' laws effectively. Nor could they
easily deal with Klan violence. When Klan suspects were arrested,
witnesses were usually reluctant to testify and Klansmen were ready to
perjure themselves to provide one another with alibis. If there was a
Klansman on a jury, it was impossible to convict. Even whites
unconnected with the Klan regarded violence against blacks as
something less than a crime. Blacks found it hard to defend themselves.
The spectre of armed blacks taking the law into their own hands was
certain to enrage the white community and escalate the violence. Nor
did most governors have much confidence in the (often black) state
militias. These were always likely to come off second best if confronted
by well-armed ex-Confederate soldiers. Moreover, even the use of the
state militia against the Klan could provoke a reaction that solidified
white opposition. This happened in North Carolina where Governor
Holden (who had declared martial law and used the state militia against
the Klan) was impeached by a newly elected state legislature for
supposedly 'subverting personal liberty'. He became the first governor
in American history to be removed from office by impeachment.

While some state governors were able to deal effectively with the
Klan, others had to appeal to Washington for help. In 1870-1 Congress

passed three Force Acts, authorising President Grant to suspend habeas corpus and to use the army to break up the Klan. Heavy penalties were imposed on those who used force, bribery or intimidation to hinder or prevent anyone from voting. Grant showed he meant business, imposing martial law in nine South Carolina counties. Hundreds of suspected Klansmen were arrested, brought to trial before mainly black juries, found guilty and imprisoned. The Force Acts effectively ended much of the violence associated with the Klan.

But violence and intimidation remained after 1872, especially in Louisiana, Mississippi and South Carolina, states still under Republican control. Mounted detachments of ex-Confederate soldiers often accompanied Democrat speakers to political rallies and paraded through black areas. These shows of strength, coupled with sporadic but well-coordinated attacks on opponents, helped to weaken black and Republican morale and made it difficult for Republicans to campaign and vote in some Southern states.

7 The South 'Redeemed'

Radical reconstruction was a limited process. It many Southern states it was over almost before it began. Tennessee and Virginia were under Democrat control by 1869; North Carolina was redeemed in 1870; Georgia in 1871; Texas in 1873; Arkansas and Alabama in 1874; and Mississippi in 1875. By 1876 only Louisiana, Florida and South Carolina were still - theoretically - under Republican control. The Democrat regimes, which replaced the Republican governments, shared a commitment to reducing the political, social and economic power of blacks and to severely reducing the scope and expense of government (and thus reducing taxes).

A number of factors played a part in Republican failure in the South and there is some disagreement over their relative importance. Most historians have rightly emphasised the importance of racism - and white intimidation and terror - in defeating Southern Republicanism. But other historians see Southern Republicanism dying of its own self-inflicted wounds. They have stressed the destructive effect of factionalism within the Southern Republican parties at state and local level. Bitter internal feuds, which often centred simply on the spoils of office rather than over actual policy, were a luxury the Republicans could scarcely afford. While agreeing on the destructive effect of factionalism, different historians stress different forces at work. Many see racism as the major cause of the in-fighting. Scalawags were always reluctant allies of the blacks. Many resented the fact that, as blacks gained political experience, they became more assertive. Black demand for office led to some scalawags leaving the Republican Party. But there was also rivalry between carpetbaggers and scalawags, and between different groups of scalawags. Even black Southerners were far from united.

John Hope Franklin, without denying the importance of racism, suggested that a Republican coalition might have survived had the party been able to unite over economic and social policy. He - and other historians - have argued that the Republican Party's best chance of success was to present itself as the poor man's party, championing policies which appealed to poor whites and blacks. Some Republicans favoured this strategy but were unable to convince the party as a whole. Most Republican leaders had no wish to embark on radical policies which were likely to prevent outside capital being attracted to the South and which would end all hope of winning 'respectable' white support.

As it was, Republican fiscal policies (at state level) did not help the party's cause. Heavy taxation succeeded in driving white yeomanry away from the party. Nor were the Republicans helped by the economic depression which started in 1873. In the five years after 1872 cotton prices fell by nearly 50 per cent and many farmers were plunged into poverty. The depression dried up the region's already inadequate sources of credit, brought an abrupt halt to most railroad building, and forced into bankruptcy even such long-established bulwarks of Southern industry as the Tredegar Iron Works. Those Republican regimes still in power were usually blamed for people's misfortunes. However, given that many states had been redeemed well before the depression began, it is hard to claim that this was a major cause of Republican decline.

Some historians have suggested that Southern Republicans were betrayed by the Northern wing of the party. Certainly by 1870 relatively few Northern Republicans showed much interest in developments in the South. They offered little in the way of financial assistance, invariably opposing measures in Congress which might have helped the South but which might also have alienated the Northern electorate. At election time the Northern Republicans continued to 'wave the bloody flag' - that is to harp back to the Civil War - a sure way of alienating potential Southern white voters.

After 1867 radical influence within the Northern Republican Party declined. Many of the radical leaders died or retired from politics. But most Northern Republicans were not, nor ever had been, radicals. Many had relatively little sympathy for the plight of Southern blacks. Virtually all Republicans agreed that blacks should have equal civil and political rights. But beyond that few were prepared to go. Most felt that it was not the federal government's job to intervene too much in state affairs. By the late 1860s Republicans were far more concerned with matters of finance, taxation and government administration than with reconstruction issues. They felt the time had come to leave the South to sort out its own problems. As the bitter memories of the war faded, there was a reluctance among many Northerners to continue to coerce the South.

President Grant's government has often been blamed for lacking commitment, vigour, vision and clear aims with regard to reconstruction. This is not altogether fair. Grant had taken tough action against the Ku Klux Klan. However, he was anxious to end federal government involvement in the South. Embarrassed by the fact than a number of Republican regimes in the South were inept and venal, he was ready to build bridges to white Southerners. Two actions symbolised this desire for accommodation with the white South. In May 1872 an Amnesty Act was passed which resulted in 150,000 ex-Confederates having their rights returned. That same year the Freedmen Bureau collapsed.

In 1872 Grant easily defeated Horace Greeley, winning over 55 per cent of the popular vote. Greeley, a liberal Northerner, only won three ex-Confederate states and three border states. Southern blacks overwhelmingly voted Republican. Grant's success heartened Republicans in both North and South. It seemed that Democrat 'redemption' was not inevitable. However, Grant's second term was dominated by two issues: the severe depression which began in 1873 and lasted until 1878; and a number of serious political scandals. The scandals, which involved some of Grant's close associates and relatives, damaged the President's standing. Although Grant had been largely unaware of what was happening around him, many Americans thought he should have known. Scandals and 'hard times' diverted the government's (and most Northerners') attention from developments in the South.

In the 1874 mid-term elections, American voters turned against the party in power and the Democrats made tremendous gains. The 110 Republican majority in the House was turned into a Democrat majority of over 60 seats and the Democrats even came close to overturning Republican control in the Senate. In these circumstances, there was little that the Republican Party or Grant's administration could do in terms of embarking on new initiatives to help Southern Republicans. Actually there was little that the President or leading Republicans wanted to do to block the resurgence of the white majority in the South. Instead, as the Northern Republican Party moved in a conservative direction, there was a growing spirit of sectional reconciliation.

The last measure to help Southern blacks was the 1875 Civil Rights Act. Supposedly designed to prevent discrimination by hotels, theatres and railroads, it was little more than a broad assertion of principle and had virtually no impact in the South. Perhaps even more ominous was the fact that a number of small but important Supreme Court decisions implied that civil rights issues should be left to individual states to determine.

There is no doubt that factionalism within Southern Republican ranks and lack of Northern Republican commitment to support radical reconstruction helped the Democrat Party redeem the South. However, this should not distract attention from the fact that the end of radical reconstruction was almost inevitable given that whites - a huge majority in most Southern states - were determined to restore white supremacy.

Race became the centre of party politics in the South. The two main political parties had distinct racial identities. The Democrat Party was the white party: the Republican Party the black party. Those historians who think that a strong Southern Republican Party might have been founded upon supporting policies that appealed to poor whites and blacks are probably deluding themselves. The reality was that few poor whites identified with poor blacks.

Given that race was the dominant issue, many of the election campaigns in the South in the 1870s were ugly and few elections were conducted fairly. White Southerners organised new paramilitary groups - Rifle Clubs, Red Shirts, White Leagues - the ostensible aim of which was to maintain public order. Their real mission, however, was to overthrow the Republican governments in the South and banish blacks from public life. Unlike the Klan, these groups drilled and paraded openly: indeed, they wanted to attract the attention of blacks to their intimidatory activities. On election days, armed whites did their best to turn blacks away from the polls. While white Southerners did their best - and worst - to ensure Republican supporters did not vote, Republican leaders tried to ensure that blacks did vote - often several times! In most states, despite white intimidation, blacks continued to vote throughout the 1870s and continued to vote Republican. But the Republican Party in the South was increasingly dominated by unscrupulous manipulators who controlled the black vote for their own ends. Vote buying became so common that blacks came to expect it.

Events in Louisiana are in some ways typical of events throughout the Deep South. Every election in the state between 1868 and 1876 was marred by violence and fraud. The chief issue was always race. After 1872 two governments claimed legitimacy in Louisiana. A Republican government, elected by blacks and protected by the federal army and black militia units, was the 'legitimate' government. But a Democrat government, elected by whites, controlled the countryside. This was strong enough to organise its own 14,000-strong militia unit - the 'White League' - which targeted Republican officials for assassination. Violence was common. In April 1873 59 blacks and 2 whites were killed in a pitched battle. 30 people died in September 1874 in another battle between the White Leagues and the official state militia. In 1874 the Republican government stayed in power by throwing out the results from many Democrat areas. Grant reluctantly sent troops to prop up the unstable and corrupt Republican regime in Louisiana. But the 1,000 or so federal troops in the state could do little to control the violence.

Strangely, Grant did nothing to help the stronger and more upright Republican government in Mississippi where there were similar 'battles' and murders. Black activists were frequently gunned down. Mississippi Democrats drew what they called the 'white line'. Any white man not enrolled in a Democrat club was subject to ostracism, economic reprisals or worse. So much pressure was applied that carpetbaggers and scalawags had to leave the state or abandon their allegiance to the Republican Party. Mississippi was redeemed in 1875. Historian Eric Foner thinks Grant's failure to intervene in Mississippi was 'a milestone in the retreat from Reconstruction'. With the Mississippi election over and the threat of federal intervention past, white Southerners settled some political scores. The black state Senator Charles Caldwell was shot by whites in a tavern. When he asked to die in the open air, his assailants carried him into the street and shot him thirty times more.

8 The End of Radical Reconstruction

Even though most states had been redeemed well before, the 1876 presidential election is often seen as the symbolic end of radical reconstruction. The Republican candidate in 1876 was Rutherford B. Hayes, described (somewhat harshly!) by the writer Henry Adams as 'a third-rate nonentity'. The Democrats chose Samuel Tilden, governor of New York. Tilden promised an end to corruption and an end of government abuse of power. The Republicans called on Northerners not to hand back power to the South, urging ex-soldiers to 'vote as they shot'.

In November 1876 it was clear that Tilden, helped by the effects of the depression and the scandals that had beset Grant's second term, had won the popular vote, gaining 4,284,000 votes to Hayes' 4,037,000. However, United States presidential elections are determined by the electoral college, not by the popular vote. Tilden had 184 electoral college votes to Hayes' 165 votes. However, the voting returns from four states - Oregon, South Carolina, Louisiana, and Florida - were contested. These four states, between them, had 20 electoral college votes. If all 20 votes went to Hayes he would triumph - by one vote! If just one state went to Tilden, he would become President. There was never much doubt that Oregon's votes would eventually go to Hayes. The real problem lay in the South, where both parties claimed to have carried South Carolina, Louisiana and Florida and where rival state governments assembled.

Southern Democrats claimed, with some justification, that Republicans had manipulated the vote in the three states and that many blacks had voted umpteen times. The Republicans claimed, with equal justification, that Southern whites had used intimidatory tactics to drive blacks from the polls. It was impossible then, and it is impossible now, to know precisely how the people in the contested Southern states voted or how far Democrat intimidation offset Republican fraud. (However, it is difficult not to have some sympathy with Tilden. He probably did carry Florida and that state alone would have given him the presidency.)

The dispute lingered on over the winter of 1876-7. Some Southern politicians talked of fighting a new Civil War to ensure that Tilden became President. But behind the scenes powerful forces worked for a peaceful settlement. Tilden had no wish for an armed conflict, and

Hayes, already favourably disposed to end the corrupt Republican regimes in the South, was ready to compromise. Eventually Congress established a 15-man Commission - 5 commissioners from the Senate, 5 from the House of Representatives and 5 from the Supreme Court - to review the election returns. Eight of the commissioners were Republicans: 7 were Democrats. By votes of 8 to 7 the commission finally awarded every one of the disputed elections to Hayes.

Disputes in Congress continued. However, the so-called 1877 Compromise (or 'Bargain') finally brought an end to the crisis. Some historians think the Compromise was as important as the Compromises of 1820 and 1850. But others wonder whether anything was agreed and thus whether there ever was a 'Compromise'. Certainly, nothing was agreed in writing. The Compromise, in so far as there was one, seems to have been as follows: the Democrats agreed to accept Hayes as President: Hayes, in return, agreed to withdraw all federal troops from the South, recognise the Democrat governments in the three disputed states, appoint a Southerner to his cabinet, and (possibly) look kindly on Southern railroad interests.

Whether Hayes agreed to any of this is debatable. He claimed that he had made no concessions to the South. Whatever had - or had not - been agreed, Hayes, following his inauguration in March 1877, quickly withdrew troops from South Carolina, Louisiana and Florida - and all three states immediately fell under Democrat control. By 1877, therefore, all the ex-Confederate states had returned to white rule. Hayes continued his policy of conciliation, appointing a white Southerner to his cabinet and visiting the South on a goodwill tour. His presidency is usually seen as marking the end of reconstruction.

It should be said that Hayes's actions did not mark an abrupt change in policy: they only confirmed what had been done by Grant, or by Congress, elsewhere in the South. But the withdrawal of federal troops did mark the end of the idea, born during the Civil War, of a powerful federal state promoting the fundamental rights of all American citizens. In Foner's view this did 'mark a major turning point in national policy'. Henceforward, Southern whites enjoyed a free hand in terms of managing Southern domestic affairs. Many Northerners, delighted that the presidential crisis was resolved, were also delighted that Southern government was back in white hands.

9 Did Reconstruction Succeed or Fail?

Historians continue to debate whether reconstruction should be regarded as a success or a failure. Much depends on which particular group is considered - white Southerners, black Southerners, Northerners - and when.

In some respects reconstruction can be seen as a success for Southern whites. Given the magnitude of the Civil War, the North had been remarkably generous. Most Southerners, even those who had held high office in the Confederacy, were quickly pardoned. Only one man, Henry Wirtz, held responsible for the horrors of Andersonville prison camp, was executed for war crimes. Jefferson Davis spent two years in prison but was then freed. White Southerners quickly resumed economic and political control. Slavery apart, there was no major confiscation of 'rebel' property. For decades to come, the Democrat Party, the political agency of white supremacy, controlled the South.

However, white Southerners had not escaped from the war scot-free. Control had been wrested away from them for a few years and they had been forced to endure something akin to military rule. Moreover, in the USA as a whole, after 1865 there was a major reduction of Southern political influence. The Southern planter class particularly lost power, both in Washington and in the South. Emancipation and the decline of Southern land values resulted in the planters also losing much of their wealth.

The main debate about reconstruction over the last three or four decades has been the effect it had on the ex-slaves. The usual claim is that reconstruction was not radical enough, that it was at best a half-finished revolution, and that as a result black Americans lost out. One major criticism was - and is - that the freedmen came out of slavery with little or no land. Those who did manage to acquire property during or at the end of the war were usually quickly dispossessed. By the 1870s most blacks eeked out a living as sharecroppers, which some see as a new type of slavery. Perpetually in debt, blacks had little economic independence. Land redistribution, it is claimed, would have had profound consequences for Southern society, protecting blacks from economic exploitation and affecting their very concept of themselves.

However, by no means all historians are so critical. They point out that major land redistribution in late nineteenth-century America was never really a viable option. In the eyes of most Americans property was sacrosanct. Most Republicans believed that black Americans should simply be provided with the opportunity to help themselves: to spoon feed them would simply destroy their character. Moreover, massive confiscation of land would have left white Southerners even more embittered. Had freedmen been given small plots of land, this would hardly have solved the economic plight of black families because falling cotton prices would probably have forced most to sell their land - as many white yeoman farmers were forced to do in the 1870s.

While accepting that black opportunities were limited, recent historians have been rather more positive about the economic impact of reconstruction on the lives of black Americans. Emancipating the slaves resulted in the greatest redistribution of income in American history. Despite efforts by whites to control ex-slaves through intimidation and violence, blacks had far more control over their own destinies and day-to-day lives than they had had under slavery. Many succeeded in buying land or negotiating contracts that freed them from direct white supervision. Sharecropping was a significant improvement over slavery. In the decades after 1865 black farmers slowly but surely increased the amount of land they farmed - and did so at the expense of white farmers. The material wealth of most freedmen improved and did so despite the adverse economic conditions of the 1870s. With the end of slavery, blacks also had mobility. Many moved to Southern cities: in the five years after 1865 the black population of the South's ten largest cities doubled. Spurred by the growth of black colleges and the development of segregated neighbourhoods, a black professional and entrepreneurial class slowly expanded. While most blacks remained in the South, some did move to the Northern cities or out West. Black cowboys were more common than Hollywood films once implied!

The second major criticism that historians have levied against reconstruction is that it failed to guarantee black Americans basic civil rights. By the first decade of the twentieth century, despite the 14th and 15th Amendments, segregation was a fact of Southern life. Every Southern state introduced segregation laws, usually known as 'Jim Crow' laws. Moreover, by about 1900 black Americans had effectively been disfranchised. State governments introduced a variety of measures - poll tax tests, literacy tests and residence requirements - to ensure that blacks were unable to vote.

However, the situation was rather more complex than historians have sometimes inferred. In his book, *The Strange Career of Jim Crow*, Vann Woodward argued that segregation was not really imposed in the South until the 1890s. Before that, in Vann Woodward's view, there was 'an era of experimentation and variety in race relations'. But this view, long accepted by historians, has now been challenged - so much so that Vann Woodward himself has conceded that segregation was the norm in most aspects of Southern life in the 'classic' reconstruction era (i.e. 1865-77). Schools, churches, transport, cemeteries, entertainment, sport, restaurants, housing, and public facilities were all effectively segregated (sometimes by law) in virtually every Southern state. It is true that a rigid legalised segregation system did not exist in every state until the 1890s. But the 1890s' laws did not represent a shift in the actual degree of segregation. What was important about the 1890s' 'Jim Crow' laws was not their newness but the relentless way that they confirmed Southern segregation.

In 1896 the Supreme Court, in the Plessy v Ferguson case, recognised that segregation was fair provided that blacks and whites had equal facilities. This judgement has often been condemned because it has been misunderstood. The Northern-dominated Supreme Court did not necessarily approve of Southern segregation. It simply thought there was little it could do to end it. Its aim was not to ensure that blacks were treated as second-class citizens. Instead, it hoped to end the unequal treatment of Southern blacks. 'Separate but equal' could be seen as an improvement over exclusion or absence.

Moreover, segregation was not something which was always imposed on blacks by vindictive Southern whites. By no means all blacks were committed to integration. Quite naturally, given their experiences under slavery, many Southern blacks had no wish to mix socially with whites. Like most American ethnic groups, they preferred to keep themselves to themselves. As a result, segregation was often simply a statement of black community identity. After 1865 there was an almost total black withdrawal from white churches as blacks tried to achieve self-determination. Churches - the first, and perhaps the most important, social institutions to be fully controlled by blacks - became a focal point of black life. Blacks also established their own welfare institutions, burial societies, Masonic lodges, temperance clubs, trade associations, political organisations, and benevolent and fraternal societies. The fact that there were black institutions, paralleling those of whites, meant there were opportunities for blacks to lead and manage.

Many blacks viewed the situation in a similar way to the Supreme Court in 1896. The real issue was not segregation as such but equal treatment within a segregated society. Separate schools were infinitely preferable to no schools at all. Ironically, in a South committed to black inferiority, the idea (and occasionally the reality) of separate but equal treatment was actually one of the achievements of reconstruction. Segregation is not necessarily the same as discrimination. It is also worth remembering that effective disfranchisement of blacks did not occur on a major scale until the 1890s. For most of the 1870s and 1880s blacks continued to vote in large numbers and continued to be appointed to public office.

However, revisionism should not be taken too far. In the South, both during and after reconstruction, blacks were regarded - and treated - by most whites as second-class citizens. Black facilities were generally markedly inferior to white. Blacks were more likely to be illiterate, more likely to live in wretched housing and more likely to suffer from malnutrition. They were also taught to know their place. There were increasingly tight local laws, similar to the 'black codes'. Savage punishments were meted out to blacks who committed petty crime and blacks were all but excluded from the machinery of law enforcement. There was considerable intimidation - physical, pyschological and economic. 'Uppity' blacks were likely to receive brutal treatment. Lynchings were a common aspect of Southern life in the late nineteenth and early twentieth centuries. (The fact that some of those who were lynched were guilty of horrendous crimes should perhaps be noted.)

Some black leaders, most notably Booker T. Washington, accepted the fact that blacks were second-class citizens. Washington argued that blacks must seek to better themselves through education and hard work. Only by so doing could they 'prove' their worth to white Americans. Given white attitudes, Washington thought that blacks had little alternative but slow, steady self-improvement. Washington's faith in education was shared by many Southern blacks. Before the Civil War over 90 per cent of the Southern adult black population was illiterate. After 1865 many black communities made great financial sacrifices, raising money to build their own schools and to pay teachers' salaries. Individuals, young and old, made similar sacrifices to educate themselves. At first most teachers were white: many were Northern school 'ma'ams' - young, middle-class and idealistic. But blacks wanted to control their own education and after 1870 most teachers in black schools and Colleges were themselves black.

It is difficult to generalise about black education in the South. Many different organisations were involved in establishing schools and there was great variation in teaching. Black schools have sometimes been criticised for trying to ape the white school system and for stressing middle-class values like self-discipline, temperance and respect for authority. But this twentieth-century criticism was rarely expressed by late nineteenth-century blacks, most of whom saw nothing wrong with 'Victorian values' and most of whom regarded education as essential for self-improvement. Enough blacks did improve themselves to suggest that some twentieth-century historians have misread the situation. Despite the decreasing amount of money spent on schools by Democrat state governments, black education was one of the great successes of reconstruction.

Southern blacks were not just victims or objects to be manipulated: they were also important participants in the reconstruction process. Individually and collectively after 1865, they sought autonomy and with some success. By the late 1860s - at work, in family relations, in education and in religion - they were free of white control. Most blacks, accepting the late nineteenth-century value system, strove by hard-work, thrift and sobriety to achieve success and prosperity. And many (although not enough) succeeded in their main goal of becoming independent landowners. Thanks to the new, segregated universities, a small but growing number of blacks became doctors, lawyers and teachers.

Black men participated more directly than black women in the struggle for freedom. This simply reflected the situation at the time. Women, whether black or white, were not expected - or allowed - to 'lead', vote, hold office or serve on juries. Male leaders of black (and white) communities - preachers, politicians, editors - promoted a strongly patriarchal view of women's role. Women's responsibility was the home: here they had some power (although they were generally urged to submit to their husbands' authority). Most black women, like most white women, shared a passionate commitment to the stability of family life. Although sharecropping soon forced many black females back to labouring on the land, they were still able to devote more time than had been possible under slavery to caring for their children and to domestic responsibilities.

In the context of the 1860s and 1870s reconstruction should be seen as radical - even revolutionary. (This in part explains the Southern white response to the process.) Dramatic changes did occur in black lifestyles. The essential fact was that blacks were no longer slaves. Most left slavery with perhaps a rather more realistic opinion of what was achievable than many twentieth-century historians. Most blacks took racial segregation for granted. Nevertheless they still viewed the new situation as one of hope and opportunity and in the years after 1865 black pride and self-esteem increased. In the late 1860s and early 1870s the freedmen demanded fair treatment and equal rights and sought to assert and defend their interests, rights and community institutions. If reconstruction did not create an integrated society, it did establish the concept of equal citizenship and a recognition of blacks' right to a share of state services. Although blacks did not emerge from reconstruction as equal citizens, at least the 14th and 15th Amendments were enshrined in the constitution. Although largely ignored in the South by the first decade of the twentieth century, the 14th and 15th Amendments were to be invoked by later generations of Civil Rights activisits.

Abraham Lincoln, who throughout the war had articulated the views of most Northern Republicans, might well have been satisfied with the results of reconstruction. The Union was restored. The scars of Civil War quickly healed. There was remarkably little 'malice'. White Southerners, for the most part, committed themselves to the Union. The position of Southern blacks had improved. And the icing on the cake for Lincoln might well have been that the Republican Party, for the most part, dominated the presidency and Congress down to 1932.

Making notes on *'Reconstruction in the South'*

Your notes on this chapter (and the last) should give you an understanding of the process of reconstruction in the South and also enable you to assess whether you think reconstruction succeeded or failed. As you read the chapter try to decide whether my view - that it was almost inevitable that the South would be 'redeemed' - is right. What could the Southern Republican governments have done that was different? What, if anything, could have saved the radical regimes? I also suggest that reconstruction was more a success than a failure. What is my main evidence for this? Does this evidence convince you? To help you make your judgement, you might be well advised to organise your notes as follows:

1   Was reconstruction a success or failure for Southern whites?
2   Was it a success or failure for Southern blacks?
3   Was it a success or failure from the point of view of most Northerners?

Answering essay questions on 'Reconstruction in the South'

It is likely you will use evidence from the last two chapters to answer specific questions about the extent to which reconstruction can be considered a success or a failure. Three typical examples of such questions are:

1 'The principles for which the Civil War was fought were sacrificed after 1865.' Discuss.
2 How far did the achievements of reconstruction fulfil its aims?
3 'A tragedy for the nation.' Is this a fair judgement on reconstruction between 1865 and 1877?

All these questions are of the same basic type. They require you to construct a two part answer. One part argues 'Yes ... principles were sacrificed/reconstruction did not fulfil its aims/was a tragedy ... in these ways/to this extent'. The other part argues 'No ... principles were not sacrificed/reconstruction did fulfil its aims/was not a tragedy... in these ways/to this extent'.

Look at question 1. First decide what were the main principles for which the war was fought. Then make a list of reasons to support the argument that those principles were sacrificed. Then make a second list of reasons to support the view that those principles were not sacrificed. Decide whether you will argue in support of the quote or against it. Now that you have an essay plan, the time has come to write the essay! Remember it is often good tactics to present the arguments you do not really agree with first; you can then use the second part of the essay to say why not, and to put forward the arguments you favour. Try to present a balanced and reasoned answer but do not be afraid to 'come off the fence' - providing you can support your view with sound evidence and display an awareness of the arguments of the other 'side'.

Many of the points made in answering question 1 would obviously be used in answering questions 2 and 3. However, the information is likely to be arranged very differently with different emphases on different areas. The introductions and conclusions of all the essays should certainly be very different. Write down a possible introductory paragraph for questions 2 and 3. In what ways are they different? In what ways are they the same? Now do exactly the same with the concluding paragraphs. Remember that while at the start of an essay you may outline an argument, in the conclusion you must be much more precise - and must answer the question set.

Source-based questions on 'Reconstruction in the South'

1 The Barrow Plantation

Examine the maps of the Barrow Plantation on page 46. Answer the following questions:
a) What do the maps indicate of the changes in black life wrought by emancipation? (5 marks)
b) What other primary sources might give the historian more information about the changes in black life on the Barrow Plantation? (5 marks)
c) To what extent do you think the changes on the Barrow Plantation were typical of changes across the Deep South? (5 marks)

2 The Ku Klux Klan

Read the extract of the Klan's 'Organisation and Principles' on pages 48-9 and examine the cartoon on this page. Answer the following questions:
a) Comment on the way that the Klan saw itself. (5 marks)
b) Comment on the way that the Klan was seen by the cartoonist. (5 marks)
c) What was the White League? (2 marks)
d) Comment on the Klan titles. (3 marks)

The White League and the klan

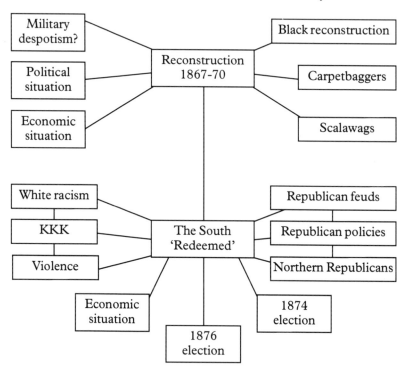

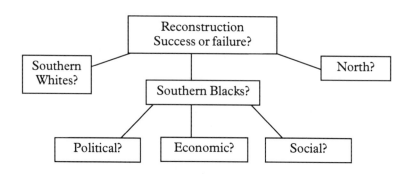

Summary - Reconstruction in the South

CHAPTER 4

The Northern Economy and Society, 1865-77

1 Introduction

Northerners spent a generation wrestling with the gigantic problems of slavery, war and reconstruction. Ironically, while they were struggling (in vain) to make Southern society a carbon copy of their own, their own society was being transformed. The social and economic world for which some Northerners fought - increasingly industrial but still predominantly agricultural, a society of small units, individual enterprise and open opportunity - did not long survive the war. Within two decades of 1865 the North had industrialised and urbanised on such a scale that the USA had became the world's pre-eminent economic power. This had a major effect on all aspects of American life. Indeed the history of late nineteenth-century America can be treated as a 'response to industrialisation'.

'In April 1861,' James Garfield (a future President) told the House of Representatives in 1868, 'there began in this country an industrial revolution ... as far-reaching in its consequences as the political and military revolution through which we have passed.' Garfield, like many of his contemporaries, believed that the Civil War had had a beneficial effect on the Northern economy. Many historians have echoed Garfield's view and seen the war accelerating the process of industrialisation. The so-called 'progressive' historians of the early twentieth century went further. They saw the Civil War as essentially a struggle between plantation agriculture on the one hand and industrialising capitalism on the other. It was not primarily a conflict between North and South: 'Merely by the accidents of climate, soil and geography was it a sectional struggle,' wrote Charles Beard, the leading progressive historian. Nor, in Beard's view, was the war a contest between slavery and freedom. Slavery just happened to be the labour system of plantation agriculture, just as wage labour happened to be the system of Northern industry. The real issues between Northern manufactures and Southern planters before the war were, according to Beard, the tariff, government subsidies to transportation and manufacturing, and public land sales. Having triumphed in the war, Northern industrialists were in a position to determine the economic development of the USA thereafter. In Beard's view, it was the economic results of the Civil War which made it America's 'second revolution'.

However, few historians today accept Beard's thesis in its entirety. While accepting that the agricultural South and the industrialising North did have different economic interests in 1861, few scholars believe that the Civil War was essentially a struggle between agrarianist and industrialist forces. Moreover, many historians now doubt whether the war had much impact on the process of industrialisation. They point out that the North was well on its way toward becoming an industrial region with a widespread factory system, an integrated railroad system, and an industrial working class before 1861. Indeed it was Northern industry which had ensured that Union forces had been able to defeat the Confederacy. Rather than encouraging, the Civil War may well have slowed down, industrial growth. After 1865 it was natural enough for Americans (like Garfield) to believe that the war had helped the USA's industrial progress, and that the terrible bloodshed had thus served a vital purpose. This belief, however, is not proof that the war actually did accelerate the process of industrialisation. This chapter is concerned with three issues: the impact the Civil War had on the Northern economy; the reasons why the North industrialised so rapidly after 1865; and the nature and extent of the social effects of that rapid industrialisation.

2 The Effect of the Civil War

It was once accepted that the Civil War was the great divide separating modern industrial America from pre-war rural society. Industrialisation, it was claimed, derived its main stimulus from the Civil War itself. The demands of the war were seen as encouraging a take off in economic growth. Moreover, the wartime legislative programme of the Republicans was thought to have unleashed business, allowing it to guide and continue the industrialising process. A case can certainly be made for the war having important short - and long - term effects on the Northern economy. That case would be as follows.

While economic devastation stalked the South, for many Northerners the Civil War was a time of unprecedented prosperity. Nourished by wartime inflation, the profits of industry boomed, as did income from speculative ventures in the stock and gold markets. Since the outbreak of the war, Senator Henry Wilson observed in 1867, 'the loyal states have accumulated more capital, have added more to their wealth, than during any previous seven years in the history of the country'. While most branches of industry prospered, those that were most closely tied to the war effort expanded most rapidly. Railroads thrived on carrying troops and supplies. On a tide of demand from the army, the meat-packing industry boomed. Chicago, the city of railroad and slaughterhouse, experienced massive growth in population, construction, banking and manufacturing. By 1865 it stood unchallenged as the Midwest's preeminent commercial centre. Agriculture also flourished. Even as farm boys by the thousands were drawn into the army, the frontier of cultivation pushed westward, with machinery and immigration replacing lost labour, and grain production and farm income continuing to grow.

In the six decades before 1861 the federal government had rarely intervened in economic matters. With the coming of war all that was to change. Congress now adopted unprecedented economic measures in an effort to promote industrial expansion and to impose organisation upon a decentralised economy. To mobilise the Union's financial resources, the government created a national paper currency (greenbacks), an enormous national debt, and a national banking system. To raise funds, the federal government increased the tariff and imposed new taxes on nearly every branch of production and consumption. To help compensate for the drain of men into the army, a federal bureau was established to encourage immigration. To promote agricultural development, the Homestead Act offered free land to settlers on the public domain, and the Land Grant College Act assisted individual states in establishing 'agricultural and mechanical colleges'. Congress also lavished enormous grants of public land and government bonds upon internal improvements, most notably the transcontinental railroad which was completed in 1869.

Without the war - and the absence of Southern representatives in Congress - the majority of these measures would have been inconceivable. Once in place, it can be claimed, each had a consequence that reverberated throughout Northern society, shifting the balance of economic power, and creating the modern American state. The high tariffs worked to the benefit of the industrial sector by protecting American industry from foreign competition. The issuance of over $400 million in paper money, (an extraordinary exercise of federal authority in a country that had never had a national currency) sparked a rapid increase in prices that inflated profits and reduced real wages, thus redistributing income upward in the social scale. Thanks to a national advertising campaign organised by Jay Cooke, who recruited a small army of agents to market government securities and invoked God and country to make their purchase seem a patriotic duty, perhaps one million Northerners ended up owning shares in a national debt that by the war's end amounted to over $2 billion. But most bonds were held by wealthy individuals and financial institutions, who reaped the windfall from interest being paid in gold at a time when depreciating paper money was employed for virtually all other transactions.

In order to create a guaranteed market for these bonds, the federal government established a national banking system. A series of laws provided for the granting of federal charters, including the right to issue currency, to banks holding specified amounts of bonds. A tax of 10 per cent on each dollar effectively ended the printing of money by state-chartered banks. The minimum capital requirement of $50,000 restricted banks to large cities. The system promoted the consolidation of a national capital market essential to future investment in industry and commerce.

Many industrialists benefited from the war. The profit boom enabled manufacturers to liquidate long-standing debts, thereby establishing their independence of merchant capital and achieving full control of their own operations. The very size of wartime profits permanently affected the scale and financing of business enterprise, channeling income into the hands of men prepared to invest in economic expansion. In 1865 Senator John Sherman of Ohio wrote to his brother, the famous general, 'The truth is the close of the war with our resources unimpaired gives an elevation, a scope to the ideas of leading capitalists far higher than anything ever undertaken in this country. They talk of millions as confidently as before of thousands'. The war may have encouraged producers and merchants to think more than ever in terms of a national market. Throughout the business world, the war may have helped to create a new type of entrepreneur with the vision and confidence to 'think big'. After the war, men such as John D. Rockefeller and Andrew Carnegie went on to revolutionise American industry.

Such are the main arguments for the war having a catalytic impact on the process of Northern industrialisation. But just as strong a case can be made for suggesting that, far from advancing industrialisation, the Civil War actually retarded it. A batch of indices of industrial activity indicate that in the 1860s the Northern economy grew more slowly than in preceding and succeeding decades. This is not surprising. The war resulted in the loss of Southern and overseas markets and dislocation to many industries, especially cotton textiles. In some vital industries, productivity increased only moderately. Pig iron production, for example, had increased by 17 per cent in the period 1855-60. It only grew by 1 per cent between 1860 and 1865. In the five years after 1865, it increased by 100 per cent. The main reason for the poor iron performance was that railroad investment declined sharply during the Civil War. Indeed, apart from the woollen industry, it is difficult to find any industry where there was accelerated growth during the war. In the industrial states of Massachusetts and New York the real value of manufacturing output declined considerably. Federal expenditure to prosecute the war failed to compensate industry for the dislocation and interruption to the economy associated with the military mobilisation of hundreds of thousands of men. Moreover, the great increase in the national debt severely contracted the possibilities for private investment in the war years.

It is also hard to prove that the Civil War had long-term catalytic effects on the Northern economy. The American industrial revolution had started well before the Civil War. The war was not a capitalist-feudal struggle, whatever Charles Beard and the 'progressive' historians might have thought. Industrial capitalism did not triumph because of the war. Indeed, it is more accurate to argue that the North triumphed in the war because of industrial capitalism. The North won the war largely because industrially it out-produced the South. It is also misleading to suggest that the North's war-time economic policy reflected a comprehensive plan to chart the course of future growth. It aimed first and foremost to mobilise the nation's resources in order to finance, fight and win the conflict. Moreover, the war-time measures were hardly revolutionary: most had long enjoyed broad support in the North and might well have been enacted even in peacetime. Government aid for the building the great transcontinental railroad, for example, simply continued the encouragement to railroads long offered by state and federal governments.

Strangely, the war generated few innovations, even in weapon production. Most manufacturing remained organised on a small-scale basis. Indeed, thousands of small firms sprang up to ride the crest of wartime profits and even traditional craft production experienced a renewed lease of life. The war, therefore, did not immediately result in the rise of big business. Indeed, it is doubtful if the war caused any fundamental economic change which would not otherwise have occurred. The North's rapid industrialisation after 1865 was certainly not the simple and direct product of wartime legislation. It is over dramatic to argue that in four years the war transferred effective economic and political power into the hands of a few industrial capitalists. This movement was already under way before 1861.

Nor was the wartime increase in tariffs new. The USA had long had protective tariffs. Economic historians continue to debate whether the high tariffs (which remained for the rest of the nineteenth century) benefited or hindered American industrial growth. American industry had grown rapidly with lower tariffs in the 1840s and 1850s. High tariffs possibly enabled American industrialists to increase profits and to pay their workers higher wages. But this was at the expense of American consumers who had to pay more for American manufactured goods.

So many influences were at work in the economy that all the Civil War claims are doubtful. But what is certain is that, even if the war did stimulate American industrial growth, there were other important and longer-term forces at work, not least the extension of the railroads, the opening of new lands out West, and Europe's growing demand for food. Two other things are clear. First, Northerners in general did not suffer as Southerners suffered. The North escaped the devastation which it helped inflict on the South. Second, the Civil War produced no massive upheaval in the Northern economic and social order equivalent to the effect of the emancipation of the slaves in the South.

3 Industrial Expansion Post-1865: an Overview

In 1865 the North was still essentially a farming section. While industry was increasing in importance, the typical manufacturing establishment remained a small workshop owned by an individual or family. Water power still equalled steam as an energy source. Within two decades of 1865, the situation had changed. A new industrial society, associated with complex technology, huge mills and factories, giant corporations and teeming cities, had emerged. It is far too simple to say that this transformation of society was the result of the Civil War: a variety of inter-related factors were at work.

Perhaps the main basis of industrialisation was the United States' abundant natural resources, especially out West (see chapter 6). The USA possessed huge deposits of coal (which increasingly powered most of the machines), iron, lead, copper, oil and great timber forests. Possession of raw materials, however, is not a sufficient explanation for the USA's industrial progress. Had this been the case, Russia would have had an equally strong economy - and this was not the case in the late nineteenth century. Obviously the USA's Western resources had to become accessible. Improvements in the nation's transportation and communication systems, especially the building of great railroad networks, helped assist the process of territorial expansion. Railroad building also created a massive demand for industrial products, particularly iron, steel and coal. Federal government support for business, both during and after the Civil War, manifesting itself in high protective tariffs, grants of land and money to railroad companies, and banking legislation, helped create a climate in which industrial capitalism could flourish. Foreign - especially British - capital also assisted development. So did the USA's increase of population. In 1860 there

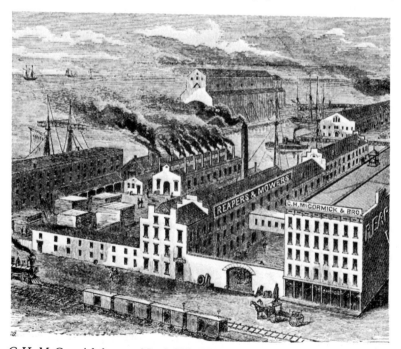

C.H. McCormick factory, North Side Chicago, 1868

were some 31 million Americans: by 1880 the population had risen to 50 million. Part of this increase was natural: Americans had large families and the death rate was declining. But immigration was another factor: no less than 2.5 million Europeans arrived in America in the 1870s. The rising population ensured a growing domestic market. Immigrants also provided a seemingly inexhaustible supply of cheap labour.

Broad social and cultural influences, especially the emphasis American society placed on hard work, thrift and acquisitiveness, may have helped encourage industrial growth. So too did rapid advances in science and technology. After 1865 Americans invented or adopted a host of new machines and industrial processes, stimulating every branch of the economy. In industry after industry, machines replaced people. Manufacturers particularly made use of two techniques of production which were essential to high volume output: continuous processing; and the use of standardised, interchangeable parts.

The dominant tendency of post-war economic organisation was consolidation of competing enterprises into large-scale units. Great entrepreneurs introduced the most advanced technology, which led to an enormous increase in productivity. There was constant pressure on firms to compete by cutting costs and prices. Eliminating rivals was part of the game.

However, American industrial expansion was not as simple as the paragraphs above suggest. In 1865 there were problems in making the economic transition from war to peace. A federal budget of almost one billion dollars in 1865 was cut savagely in 1866. 1.5 million men, who had been directly or indirectly engaged in prosecuting the war, were released to the work force, which in addition had to absorb a stream of 300,000 immigrants in both 1866 and 1867. In consequence, there was a short-lived contraction - 'slump' would be too strong a word - from April 1865 until December 1867. This was followed by a period of great prosperity. By 1873 American industrial production stood 75 per cent above its 1865 level. But in 1873 a severe depression - one of the most serious in American history - set in, lasting until the end of the 1870s. By 1879 some 13 per cent of the work force were unemployed.

However, the term 'depression' is somewhat misleading because it implies a general contraction in economic activity. In fact, in many industries output continued to expand rapidly. This was largely because of new processes, new technology, new sources of raw material, and improved communications. Developments in the iron and steel industry - an essential element in the industrialisation process - are indicative of developments in other industries. After 1865 pig iron production soared. In the 1870s the great iron fields rimming Lake Superior started to yield their treasures. By 1880 iron output had reached 4.3 million tons, compared with 920,000 tons in 1860. Steel production increased even more rapidly. This was largely due to the Bessemer process - invented by the Englishman Henry Bessemer and an American William

Kelly virtually simultaneously. This process - a cheap and practical way of ridding molten pig iron of carbon, phosphorus and other impurities - first went into operation in the USA in 1864. In 1868 another and superior method of oxidising the impurities in iron - the open hearth process - a joint discovery by German and French inventors - was introduced. The new processes cut production costs, enabling manufacturers to boost production and reduce the price of steel. Hitherto, steel had been used for making small and expensive articles. In 1870 only 77,000 tons of steel were manufactured - less than 4 per cent of the volume of pig iron. By 1880 some 1.4 million tons were produced. American iron and steel mills, centred on Pittsburgh, Cleveland, Detroit, Gary and Chicago, were more efficient than their British counterparts. The new iron and steel business, which required expensive equipment, a large labour force and financial reserves to withstand the buffeting of hard times, was ill-suited to small-scale operators. The postwar years - and particularly the depression years after 1873 - resulted in consolidation in iron and steel production. One of the greatest producers was the Andrew Carnegie syndicate (see pages 78-9). By 1880 Carnegie's company was turning out 25 per cent of the USA's steel ingots.

The petroleum industrial expansion - and consolidation - was even more spectacular than that of iron and steel. The first successful oil well began business in Pennsylvania in 1859. In the Civil War production ranged between 2 and 3 million barrels per year. By 1873 about 10 million barrels a year were produced. The most important petroleum product was kerosene - a fuel used in lamps. In the 1860s there were hundreds of tiny refineries all over Pennsylvania. The business was chaotic and vigorously competitive with barrel prices rising as high as $13.75 and falling as low as 10 cents. In general, as more oil was found, output exceeded demand and companies were involved in a brutal struggle to survive. Technological advances came rapidly, especially in oil refining - a safer and more profitable business than simple oil-production. Larger plants, using expensive machinery and employing skilled technology, had all the advantages. By the 1870s John D. Rockefeller's Standard Oil Company of Ohio had emerged as the giant among refiners, exploiting every possible new technological advance and employing fair measures and foul to force its competitors to sell out or join forces. By 1879 over 90 per cent of the USA's oil refining capacity was in Rockefeller's hands.

4 Railroads

Railroads had developed early in the USA. Indeed most of the features associated with late nineteenth-century railroads were developed in the railroad boom of the 1850s and arguably there was no great change after 1865. Historian Robert Fogel has gone so far as to claim that railroads did not make 'an overwhelming contribution' to the USA's economic development, arguing that the canal and road network could have sustained American industrial expansion. His arguments are not convincing. In reality, railroads were a vital element in the USA's post-war economic growth and constituted the most important single economic interest in the USA. In 1865 the USA had under 35,000 miles of track: by 1880 this had increased to over 90,000 miles. By sharply reducing transportation costs, railroads played a major role in Western settlement as well as making possible the exploitation of natural resources and the creation of a vast national market. Railroad needs, moreover, largely accounted for the great expansion of coal and steel production. By 1880 railroads consumed over 90 per cent of all the rolled steel manufactured in the USA.

Railroad building occurred in every part of the USA (see pages 119-22 for Western development). In the North-east the major emphasis was on filling in the gaps and on developing integrated trunk routes. Hundreds of small lines were consolidated by lease, purchase, or merger into a handful of large systems, so that long-distance travellers no longer needed to make frequent changes of train. Increased amalgamation eased the adoption of a uniform gauge of 4 feet 8 and a half inches, virtually achieved by the mid-1880s. Technological advances made rail travel safer and less of an ordeal. An enterprising New Yorker, George Pullman, who had introduced the sleeping-car during the Civil War, founded the Pullman Palace Car Company in 1867. The next year he launched the first dining car and soon produced parlour and drawing-room cars. The introduction of air brakes, patented in 1869, improved safety standards. Air brakes also made possible a massive increase in the size of trains and the speed at which they could safely operate. To pull heavier trains, more powerful locomotives were needed. This, in turn, produced a demand for steel rails which were much stronger and more durable than iron rails.

Railroads were America's first big businesses, the first magnet for the great financial markets. Railroad companies' voracious appetite for funds absorbed most of the nation's investment capital (leaving little available for the credit-hungry South), contributed to the development of banking, and facilitated the further concentration of the nation's capital market in Wall Street. After 1865 a few big companies devoured scores of smaller companies to create large, integrated networks. Under the aggressive leadership of Thomas Scott, Pennsylvania Railroad became the USA's largest corporation - an economic empire of over 6,000 miles of track stretching across the continent. Only two nations, Britain and France, possessed more track than Scott's company. Railroad companies far outstripped the largest manufacturing concerns in capital, operating expenses, and number of employees. Railroads pioneered crucial aspects of large-scale enterprise. Most companies set up clearly defined hierarchical organisation structures and divided their lines into separate geographical units with armies of professional managers overseeing far-flung activities. Companies also set up separate departments to handle finance and document the cost of every operation. Other departments supervised the movement of trains and the procuring of business. Railroad management operations thus became a model for other businesses seeking a national market. For entrepreneurs, railroads created opportunities for unheard of wealth, even though many railroad companies never paid a dividend and many eventually went bankrupt.

For all the benefits railroads brought, there was much to criticise in the way they were built, financed and operated. Dozens of railroad men plundered their companies by setting up their own dummy construction companies to lay the track at exorbitant prices; others cheated investors by issuing false prospectuses. Wasteful construction and over-building, beyond the needs of traffic, left many companies with a crushing burden of debt. So did stock-watering - the issuing of stock in excess of the value of the assets. The result was cutthroat competition accompanied by rate-wars and the granting of huge rebates - secret reductions below the published tariff - in order to secure the business of large customers. The shady financial practices of the railroad men earned them the label the 'robber barons', a title soon extended to great 'captains of industry' as well. Some railroad magnates, such as James Hill of the Great Northern, a man of vision and the highest financial probity, displayed a genuine concern for the regions their railroads served. But at the other extreme were men like Jay Gould and Jim Fisk who made the Erie Railroad a byword for chicanery and fraud and whose speculation finally ruined it. Gould's career encompassed almost every known variety of chicanery and nearly every enterprise he touched was either compromised or ruined. Nevertheless, when he died at the age of 56, he had amassed a personal fortune amounting to $100 million.

A more representative figure, in the sense that he was a mixture of vices and virtues, was Cornelius Vanderbilt, a cynical, crude but far-sighted New Yorker who was already a wealthy shipowner when he turned late in life to railroads. 'Commodore' Vanderbilt not only made the New York Central prosperous but improved services and equipment, and reduced rates. But he was also a ruthless competitor who was prepared to corrupt legislators and manipulate stock for his own benefit. By the time of Vanderbilt's death in 1877, the New York Central operated a network of over 4,500 miles of track and the 'Commodore' had amassed a fortune of $90 million.

By the late 1860s there was increasing public hostility towards railroad malpractices. Criticisms centred chiefly on freight rates, especially discriminatory policies that favoured large customers at the expense of smaller competitors. There was also widespread indignation at railroad attempts to 'influence' newspaper editors and public officials by outright bribery. Starting with Massachusetts in 1869, a number of eastern states established advisory railroad commissions of nonpartisan experts. While lacking coercive power and having no direct authority over railroad policies, the commissions investigated complaints, collected statistics and published reports on the practices of local lines. They often had great influence: railroad companies were at pains to please them; and their recommendations carried weight with politicians and the general public. The first attempt at thorough-going state regulation came in the Mid-west as a result of agitation by farmers' organisations, especially the Granger Movement (see pages 110-11). In the 1870s Illinois, Iowa, Minnesota, Missouri, Kansas and Nebraska all passed so-called Granger laws which fixed maximum rates for passengers and freight, forbade various discriminatory practices, and established railroad commissions to enforce the regulations. Railroad companies claimed that such measures were unconstitutional because they infringed the power of Congress over interstate commerce and because rate-fixing amounted to deprivation of property, without due process of law. But in Munn v Illinois (1877) the Supreme Court held otherwise. Affirming the right of the state to regulate public utilities, Chief Justice Waite declared that when private property was devoted to public use, it 'must submit to be controlled by the public for the public good'.

Nevertheless, state regulation was not very effective. Some of the commissioners were incompetent and a few were corrupt. Regulations were often loosely drawn and the railroad companies often successfully challenged them in the courts. Separate state action also meant a confusing miscellany of different rate structures. Somewhat ironically, the commissions often found that most companies were not over-charging and that most rates were as low as could be expected. Indeed by 1876, as a result of rate wars, many railroad companies were near bankruptcy.

5 Inventions

A flood of inventions and technological innovations accompanied - indeed made possible - the process of industrialisation. If Europeans made most of the key scientific discoveries on which American technology was based, Americans proved readier to apply them. But Americans themselves were extraordinarily inventive. The number of patents soared from an annual average of 2,000 in the 1850s to 13,000 in the 1870s. Many were trivial improvements; others were impracticable or hair-brained. But the volume of patents was a significant yardstick of the USA's economic progress.

New processes were introduced in almost every aspect of business. Dramatic improvements in communications made it possible to direct huge and widely scattered organisations and to operate on a national - and international - scale. The electric telegraph, which spanned the continent by 1862, was rapidly extended after 1865. By 1878 Western Union, which controlled 80 per cent of the telegraph business, owned 195,000 miles of telegraph routes. (The company operated along - and in conjunction with - the great railroads.) In 1866 a trans-Atlantic cable was successfully laid, ensuring that news and stock-market quotations could be transmitted instantaneously, rather than take two weeks or more to cross the ocean by steamer.

Few, if any, inventions of the times could rival the importance of the telephone, patented by Alexander Graham Bell in 1876 and demonstrated at the Philadelphia Centennial Exposition the same year. To promote the new device the inventor and his backers formed the Bell Telephone Association which became the National Bell Telephone Company in 1879. The USA was far ahead of Europe in developing a telephone network. By 1879 Bell's Company had installed some 56,000 telephones (including one in the White House) and 55 cities had local telephone networks. The typewriter also had a great impact on business life. Invented in 1867 by Christopher Latham Sholes, it was finally marketed by the Remington Gun Company. One of its first purchasers was Mark Twain whose *Adventures of Tom Sawyer,* published in 1875, is thought to be the first American novel composed on a typewriter. Soon few American business offices were without the new machine.

McCormick Advanced Self-Raking Reaper, 1869

The list of innovations was massive. New processes in steelmaking and oil refining were the foundation of the Carnegie and Rockefeller enterprises. The refrigerator car made it possible for Western beef, mutton and pork to reach a national market, giving rise to the great packing-house enterprises of Gustavus Swift in Chicago and Philip Armour in Minneapolis. New inventions (e.g. barbed wire and vacuum cleaners) and advances in technology (e.g. steam turbines and gas distribution) altered the lives of ordinary people far more than did the activities of politicians. Without doubt, the greatest inventor was Thomas Edison. Born in Ohio in 1847, Edison had little formal education. A railroad newsboy at 12 and a telegraph operator at 16, he devoted all his spare time and money to technical apparatus. In 1876 he

Year	Wheeler and Wilson	Willcox & Gibbs	Singer
1853	799	n.a.	810
1854	756	n.a.	879
1855	1,171	n.a.	883
1856	2,210	n.a.	2,564
1857	4,591	n.a.	3,630
1858	7,978	n.a.	3,594
1859	21,306	n.a.	10,953
1860	25,102	n.a.	13,000
1861	18,556	n.a.	16,000
1862	28,202	n.a.	18,396
1863	29,778	n.a.	21,000
1864	40,062	n.a.	23,632
1865	39,157	n.a.	26,340
1866	50,132	n.a.	30,960
1867	38,055	14,150	43,053
1868	n.a.	15,000	59,629
1869	78,866	17,251	86,781
1870	83,208	28,890	127,833
1871	128,526	30,127	181,260
1872	174,088	33,639	219,758
1873	119,190	15,881	232,444
1874	92,827	13,710	241,679
1875	103,740	14,502	249,852
1876	108,997	12,758	262,316

Production of Wheeler and Wilson, Willcox & Gibbs and Singer sewing machines 1853-76

Source: Frederick G. Bourne, 'American Sewing-Machines' in *One Hundred Years of American Commerce*, ed. Chauncey M. Depew

went full time into the 'invention business', establishing a research laboratory at Menlo Park, New Jersey. Hitherto most inventors, motivated by scientific curiosity, had worked singly and explored problems at random. Edison's 'invention factory' was based on the concept of organised team research. His laboratories created or perfected scores of new devices including the phonograph in 1877 and the first successful incandescent light bulb in 1879.

6 The Great Entrepreneurs

American industrialisation was marked by the rise of great entrepreneurs who were skilled in organising, promoting and ultimately dominating particular fields of industry. Like the railroad 'robber barons', they were a diverse group. Some were unsavoury characters, ready to use fraudulent practices. Others were upstanding businessmen who managed their companies with sophistication and innovation. Most were men of great energy and ability. Highly - indeed often ferociously - competitive in a highly competitive society, they were ready to gamble and seize the main chance. Most were of British descent: most were pious and religious. While they have often been maligned, their efforts helped make the USA the leading industrial nation in the world. Arguably they were more important to America's development than most of the Presidents of the period.

Two entrepreneurs stand head and shoulders above the rest: John D. Rockefeller and Andrew Carnegie. Rockefeller was associated with the oil business. After the first successful drilling in Pennsylvania in 1859, the business quickly expanded as petroleum products were used for heating, lubrication, medicine and above all lighting, with kerosene replacing tallow and whale oil. Little capital was needed for drilling or refining and soon thousands of small operators entered the business. Markets were periodically glutted and prices and profits fluctuated wildly. In consequence, the business was (violently!) competitive. Rockefeller turned his full attention to the oil business in 1865 when, aged 26, he formed a Cleveland oil refining firm. Combining superb business talent with low business ethics, he set out to win control of the industry. A consummate organiser, he insisted on sound financial practices and systematised marketing and distribution. In 1870 his firm was reorganised as the Standard Oil Company of Ohio with capital of $1 million.

Year by year, Rockefeller destroyed the opposition by buying - or driving - out competitors. Blackmail, espionage, price slashing and secret deals with railroad companies were all part of the game. By 1879 Standard Oil had come to control over 90 per cent of the oil refining in the USA and Rockefeller's petrol empire was selling a wide variety of products in every part of America and many parts of the world. Much of Rockefeller's success was based on his determination to 'pay nobody a profit'. Crude oil sources and transportation systems were acquired and huge selling organisations established so that Standard Oil was not dependent on the products or services of other firms. Rockefeller later described his methods. In 1879, he said:

1 We had taken steps of progress that our rivals could not take. They had not the means to build pipe lines, bulk ships, tank wagons; they could not have their agents all over the country; couldn't manage their own acid, bungs, wicks, lamps, do their own
5 cooperage - so many other things; it ramified indefinitely. They couldn't have their own purchasing agents as we did, taking advantage of large buying.

Eventually, in order to consolidate scattered business interests under a more efficient control, Rockefeller and his associates resorted to a new legal device - the trust. Long established in law to enable people to manage property belonging to others, such as children or the mentally incompetent, the trust now was used for another purpose - centralised control of business. Since Standard Oil of Ohio was not permitted to hold property out of state, it began in 1872 to place properties or companies acquired elsewhere, in trust, usually with the company secretary at first but later with nine trustees. The trust device was soon to be widely copied.

The growth of Rockefellers's wealth and influence, together with his apparent indifference to public opinion, led to his being widely reviled as an avaricious and coldhearted monster. He was particularly loathed by the rivals he had destroyed. Even Alan Nevins, Rockefeller's most sympathetic biographer, admitted that Standard Oil 'committed acts against competitors which could not be defended'. But in fairness to Rockefeller, he did nothing that many of his rivals were not already doing. His success was the result of meticulous attention to detail, a profound grasp of the economies of large-scale production, and good appointments of subordinates. His efforts did bring order and efficiency to the oil refining business.

Rockefeller came from a wealthy family. The same could not be said of Andrew Carnegie. Born in Scotland, the son of a poor hand-loom weaver, his family emigrated to Pennsylvania in 1848. Aged 13, Carnegie started out as a bobbin boy in a textile mill, earning $1.20 per week. At 14 he was earning $2.50 per week as a telegraph messenger. Soon he was promoted to telegrapher and in 1853 became personal secretary and telegrapher to Thomas Scott, district superintendent of the Pennsylvania Railroad. When Scott became president of the railroad, Carnegie became superintendent. When, during the Civil War, Scott became Assistant Secretary of War in charge of transportation, Carnegie worked with him. In 1865 Carnegie, already rich, quit the railroad business, determined to develop his own interests. By the 1870s he was concentrating on iron and steel production. Though without training in engineering or technology, he was quick to grasp the significance of new processes of steel manufacture. A tour of Bessemer steel plants in England in 1872 convinced him that his previous plans for expansion of the small Freedom Iron and Steel Company were much too modest: he decided instead to build an entirely new mill with the most up-to-date equipment available. To supervise construction, Carnegie hired Alexander Holley, the greatest authority on Bessemer methods in the USA, and between 1873 and 1875 built the Edgar Thompson Steel Works, the most efficient in the USA. A man of driving energy, Carnegie rode roughshod over competitors and trade unions alike, and in a business where there was merciless competition, came out on top. Like Rockefeller, he was materially assisted by the panic of 1873. In the depression that followed, Carnegie said afterwards:

So many of my friends needed money, that they begged me to repay them. I did so and bought out five or six of them. That was what gave me my leading interest in this steel business.

A promoter and organiser, Carnegie also had an enviable gift of surrounding himself with able associates like the hard-headed businessman Henry Clay Frick. He and Frick ultimately created a huge combine, embracing coalfields, limestone deposits, iron mines, ore ships and railways. By 1880 the Carnegie Company dominated the American steel industry and Carnegie himself was on his way to becoming one of the richest men on earth.

Carnegie had no difficulty justifying either his wealth or the growth of big business. Like many men at the time, he believed in the notion of the survival of the fittest: in his view it was a social and Christian duty to get rich. He thought that the great captains of industry were, on the whole, public benefactors who helped create American wealth and jobs. Many eminent politicians, intellectuals, social scientists and clergymen agreed with him, formulating a clear-cut rationale of rugged individualism, and supporting unbridled competitive struggle. Many believed the rise of the great entrepreneurs was inevitable. In 1879, William Vanderbilt, testifying before a Congressional committee, expressed the popular opinion of the time.

Yes they are very shrewd men. I don't believe that by any legislative enactment or anything else, through any of the States or all of the States, you can keep such men down. You can't do it! They will be on top all the time. You see if they are not.

Carnegie's rags-to-riches experience became a model for many Americans - native-born and immigrants alike. The notion of self-help was particularly pedalled by Horatio Alger, a Unitarian minister and writer of popular boys' novels in the years after 1865. Most of his books had similar plots. Invariably boys from poor backgrounds, as a result of ambition, initiative, integrity, thrift and hard-work, made good. Ironically, Carnegie's rise was exceptional. Most of the richest industrial leaders were from upper and middle-class backgrounds. But enough men rose to great wealth, through both luck and talent, to keep alive the 'American Dream'.

7 Urbanisation and the Standard of Living

In 1860 one in every six Americans was already a city dweller and New York was already the third largest city in the world. All of the USA's great cities (except New Orleans) were in the North. After 1865, Northern cities continued to expand so that by 1880 50 per cent of the North-east was urbanised. Railroads, heavy industry and technological advances helped build cities and were in turn stimulated by them. Not until 1920 would a majority of Americans actually live in urban areas. But by the 1870s the city had become the dominant force in Northern life.

Rural depopulation complemented urban growth. Unable to compete with Western farmers, virtually the entire North-eastern half of the USA - but particularly New England - experienced a flight from the land. The exodus to the cities was not merely the result of agricultural poverty. City life was attractive to many countrymen: urban work tended to be easier and better paid than rural work.

The population growth in American cities was also the result of immigration. Most immigrants gathered in cities simply because they lacked the means to go West and take up farms. Cheap labour was in demand in most cities so that immigrants were usually able to find work. There was the added bonus that in cities immigrants usually lived with others of like language, customs and religion.

Given that city planning was virtually unknown in the late nineteenth century, American cities grew haphazardly. Housing conditions were often appalling and over-crowded slum areas bred crime. Industrialisation also devastated the urban environment. Rivers were polluted and skies filled with clouds of soot. Mud, horse droppings and garbage befouled the streets. Rapid growth strained most services and city governments were unable to cope with problems of water supply, sewage disposal, disease, paving, lighting and policing. More heed was paid to enlarging water supplies than to sewage or industrial waste. In consequence, typhoid and other epidemics were common. (The life expectancy of males in New York city in 1880 was 29!) The situation was not helped by the fact that most city governments were massively corrupt. Political machines, often led by unscrupulous city bosses, wielded tremendous power, controlling thousands of jobs in the police and fire services, education, courts and hospitals. The operators of public utilities - gas, water and streetcars - were often forced to pay huge bribes to bosses and/or machines to obtain city franchises.

However, although municipal functions and social services became entangled with corrupt politics, this did not prevent efforts being made to improve various aspects of city life. City bosses often provided semi-welfare systems, especially for immigrants, in return for political support. Most towns improved their transport services. Street cars, pulled by horses along railway tracks, conveyed people within towns. In 1873 San Francisco became the first city to use cable cars which clamped onto a moving underground cable driven by a central power source. This system quickly spread. Most towns also developed parks. The landscape architect Frederick Law Olmsted played an important role. Appointed chief architect of New York's Central Park in 1858, he subsequently executed commissions in many other cities including Chicago and Detroit.

Cities did have their attractions. Town dwellers had a far greater choice of consumer goods and at lower prices than rural and small-town Americans. They also had more job opportunities, were paid higher wages, and had more leisure time and more varied leisure activities than people in rural areas. There was increasing mass entertainment, including circus, drama, music and sport. Baseball, a favourite army recreation during the Civil War, became the most popular spectator sport: the first professional team, the Cincinnati Red Stockings, was formed in 1869 and the National League was organised in 1876. Horse-racing and boxing were other popular sports.

It is sometimes claimed that industrialisation robbed working men and women of their status, security, independence and creative pride, and destroyed the former close relationship between employers and employees. By 1880 the occupational structure was certainly in the process of being rearranged and many craftsmen did feel threatened by the new machine age which reduced the demands for their skills. However, to those who came to factory, mill or mine work from farm labour or domestic service, changing work patterns often meant liberation from inferiority and dependence. Accompanying industrialisation and urbanisation was a rising standard of living. While the rich were getting richer and the gulf between rich and poor was widening, the poor were generally better off. While rags to riches was rare, upward mobility both from 'blue collar to white collar' and from unskilled to skilled manual jobs was common. Americans were also geographically mobile as people moved to try to better themselves.

For most Northerners the period 1865-80 was an age of increasing comfort and convenience. A host of mechanical inventions and gadgets transformed the conditions of life. The widespread use of sewing machines, for example, made available a wider variety of clothing and eased the lives of millions of women. New methods of preserving food meant that city dwellers had more varied and nutritious diets. In virtually every industry, mechanisation increased output and decreased prices. Far more was thus available for the consumer.

8 Trade Unions

Although real wages were increasing, conditions in many industries were abysmal. Workers worked long hours for low wages in conditions which were often hazardous to health and safety. A ten hour day was normal and a twelve to eighteen hour day not uncommon. As in Britain, this state of affairs encouraged the rise of trade unions. It seemed to many that only through the consolidation of labour could workingmen hope to combat the power of aggregated wealth.

Although local trade unions had existed in the USA from the late eighteenth century, they had generally had little success. In the 1850s skilled workers in trades such as printing, cigar-making and iron-working had established national associations along craft lines. By 1860 there were about 20 such craft unions and during the Civil War, because of the demand for labour, such unions grew in strength. Local unions, however, remained the norm. By 1865 such unions, composed mainly of skilled workers, existed in cities throughout the North and strikes had become a regular feature of industrial life.

After 1865 various efforts were made to create a more united labour movement. The first attempt to combine different unions into a single body with mass membership came in 1866 when William Sylvis, leader of the Iron Moulder's Union, founded the National Labour Union (NLU). The NLU comprised delegates from trade unions, farmers' associations and various middle-class reform groups who were more interested in long term political and social reform than in the immediate problems of workingmen. While espousing such ideas as a maximum eight hour day, workers' co-operatives, and equal rights for women, many of the NLU's leaders were out of touch with the practical needs and aspirations of workers. Sylvis's sudden death in 1869 had a damaging effect on the heterogeneous organisation and it collapsed in the early 1870s.

As the NLU faded, another group emerged. This was the Noble and Holy Order of the Knights of Labour. Founded by Uriah Stephens, a Philadelphia tailor, in 1869, the organisation was modelled on the Masonic Order. Secrecy, Stephens felt, along with a semi-religious elaborate ritual, would protect members against retaliation and at the same time create a sense of solidarity. His aim was to unite all 'toilers' in one grand association, irrespective of occupation, race, nationality or sex. (The only occupations excluded from the order were lawyers, bankers, liquor dealers and professional gamblers!) The Knights of Labour grew slowly. Not until the coming of the 1873 depression did it begin to make much headway. Like the NLU, it emphasised reform rather than class conflict. Stephens preferred boycotts to strikes and believed the Knights could best achieve their objectives - an eight hour day, equal pay for equal work by both sexes, and an end to child labour - through legislation and more particularly through the formation of producers' co-operatives. The Knights did not establish a national organisation until 1878 and were not to become a significant force until the 1880s.

By the 1870s most single occupational unions were still craft unions. A few, like the Iron Moulders, were national but most remained local. Strikes, which were mainly about wage levels, were commonplace. Success or failure of strike action tended to determine how long local unions survived. In the early 1870s, for example, some 50,000 Pennsylvania miners had enrolled in a Workingmen's Benevolent Association. In 1875 the miners waged a six month strike and were completely defeated. By 1876 membership of the Association had shrunk to almost nothing.

Most Unions were moderate - not revolutionary or violent. But not all. The 1870s saw a reign of terror in the eastern Pennsylvania coal fields, attributed to an Irish group, members of the Ancient Order of Hibernians, usually called the Molly Maguires. The group tried to right perceived wrongs against Irish workers by intimidation, beatings and killings. Their actions excited high emotions. Molly Maguire terrorism reached its peak in 1874-5 and mine owners hired Pinkerton detectives to infiltrate the movement. One of the agents produced enough evidence to indict the leaders. In 1876 24 of the Molly Maguires were convicted and ten were hanged for murder and conspiracy.

Of far more significance than the Molly Maguires was the Great Railroad Strike of 1877, the first major interstate strike. After 1873 all the major railroad companies had cut wages. In 1877 they made another 10 per cent cut. Incensed by the fact that the railroad companies continued to pay shareholders dividends, railroad workers at Martinsburg, West Virginia, went on strike and blocked the tracks. Without organised direction, their picketing degenerated into mob violence. The governor of West Virginia sent in the militia to get the trains moving but the militia fraternised with the strikers. Federal troops were eventually sent in and restored order. Meanwhile walkouts and sympathy demonstrations spread, soon paralysing two-thirds of the nation's rail network. In Baltimore there were pitched battles between striking workers and the forces of order, resulting in ten deaths and over 250 arrests. The most serious outbreak of violence was at Pittsburgh in July. Public sympathy for the strikers was so great that local militiamen joined rather than suppressed the striking workers. Militiamen from Philadelphia managed to disperse one crowd but were then forced to shoot their way out of trouble at a cost of 26 lives. Over a three days period, mobs of people caused about $5 million worth of damage as shops were looted and railroad property destroyed. Public opinion now turned against the strikers and order was quickly restored when President Hayes sent in federal troops armed with new machine guns. Everywhere the strike failed in the face of overwhelming state and federal force and eventually the strikers had no choice but to drift back to work without achieving any of their demands.

For many Americans, the Great Railroad Strike raised the spectre of a worker-based social revolution like the Paris Commune of 1871. There was fear of civil war between capital and labour. However, this fear was not to be realised. The reality was that most workers were not militant: few labour leaders talked of class war and many thought that strikes were anachronistic. The working classes in the USA were far from united. Most skilled workers felt little solidarity with unskilled workers and were even divided among themselves: most were loyal to their craft rather than their class. Various ethnic groups felt they had little in common with each other. Nearly all white unions, for example, barred blacks from membership. Many also viewed women as a threat to wage levels. Employers, in consequence, found it easy to play off one group against another. They could invariably find newcomers willing to work for low wages and to act as strike-breakers.

The Great Railroad Strike showed how hard it was for a trade union to control a nationwide strike. The labour movement lacked the administrative skills and unity of purpose to operate effectively on a national scale. It also faced opposition in high places. As the 1877 Strike demonstrated, political leaders respected property rights more than the rights of labour. Employers, moreover, could invariably rely on the strong bias of law courts in favour of capital. Labour leaders who used violence were often punished: employers who were prepared to use spies, blackmail and sometimes armed force to thwart union organisation were rarely brought to task.

The 1870s depression meant it was hard for workers to win wage increases from hard-pressed employers. Many workers feared losing their jobs. Others had little faith in trade unions which they saw as being somehow un-American. Many workers do not seem to have considered themselves exploited. In addition, some state governments, especially Massachusetts, enacted a sizeable body of labour legislation, designed to help workers, including limiting the working day to eight hours. Although it is hard to generalise about actual working conditions - these obviously varied from industry to industry - it appears that they marginally improved. In 1860 the average worker laboured for eleven hours a day: by 1880 only one worker in four laboured for more than ten hours. Material improvements and faith in the American dream exacerbated the problems of those who wanted to establish trade unions.

9 Social Change

The Civil War had less impact on Northern society than might have been expected.

a) The Role of Women

Women had played a major role in the Northern war effort. Some of the jobs that had previously been done by men were undertaken by women. Hundreds of thousands of women also involved themselves in voluntary war work, organising medical relief and gathering supplies for soldiers. Although men led most voluntary organisations, the war years inculcated among some women a heightened interest in public events and a sense of independence and accomplishment.

After the war, however, there was a swift return to the cult of domesticity. It was generally accepted (by men) that women's place was in the home and that women should not have equal political or legal rights. Most women seem to have accepted their lot. In 1870 less than one in five Northern women actually went out to work. Nearly all those who were gainfully employed were unmarried or widowed. Most were employed as domestic servants or factory workers. Given the stigma that was attached to being a servant in the USA, most moved into better paid and less demeaning factory work if the opportunity arose. Women were usually paid far less than men even when they did the same work. In fact, they rarely did the same work. As a rule, they worked in a narrower range of occupations and in less skilled positions than men. Even when they worked in the same industry, they did different jobs. In short the labour force had two separate work and wage tracks - one for men and one for women.

Some women chaffed against the restraints and inequalities of the system. Resenting their legal and political subordination, a few demanded the right to vote. In 1869 Anthony and Elizabeth Cady Stanton founded the National Woman Suffrage Association which, while aiming to promote a women's suffrage amendment to the constitution, looked upon suffrage as but one among many feminist causes to be promoted. Later that year, Lucy Stone, Julia Ward Howe and other leaders formed the American Woman Suffrage Association, which focused single-mindedly on the suffrage as the first and basic reform. Women's battle for the vote occurred mainly at state level and was marked more by failure than success. Nevertheless, a few states did grant women suffrage in school board or municipal elections and in 1869 the territory of Wyoming, in an effort to attract females (the territory had seven men for every woman), granted full suffrage to women. However, it was another 50 years before the female suffrage battle was won at national level.

Agitation over women's rights was largely confined to upper and middle class women who had the time to organise. But most women of this class did not campaign actively for the right to vote. They were far more likely to direct their energy towards social welfare activities, especially to the temperance cause. Others devoted themselves to charitable work. A number of women's clubs were established (for example, the Young Women's Christian Association): some clubs confined themselves to literary and social activities; but others became deeply involved in social welfare issues.

b) Northern Blacks

If the Civil War seemed to open the doors of opportunity for Northern women, it held out hope for an even more radical transformation of the condition of the black population of the free states. There were fewer than 250,000 Northern blacks in 1860 - less than 2 per cent of the North's population. Although free, they usually had the worst jobs and segregation was the norm in most aspects of life. Only three Northern states allowed blacks to vote on terms of complete parity with whites in 1860. Before the Civil War some Northern states had tried to exclude blacks altogether. However, historian Paul Finkelman has recently stressed that race relations in the ante-bellum North showed greater complexity and ambiguity than was once thought. A number of Northern politicians in the decades before the Civil War worked hard to expand black rights. By 1860 legal changes had altered the status of blacks in many Northern states. Only three states actually restricted black immigration. Almost all Northern states provided some public education for blacks and integrated schools existed in some states. In 1861 Northern blacks had more rights than at any time in the previous thirty years.

The effect of the Civil War was to continue this liberalising trend and to raise blacks' sense of optimism about the future. Throughout the war, black leaders had insisted that the logical and essential corollaries of emancipation were the end of all colour discrimination, the establishment of equality before the law and the enfranchisement of the black population. Both during and after the war, the North's official racial barriers began to fall. In 1865, for example, Illinois repealed its laws barring blacks from entering the state, serving on juries or testifying in court, while Ohio eliminated the last of its discriminatory black laws. Northern states accepted the 14th and 15th Amendment - albeit reluctantly in many instances - and by the 1870s Northern blacks (on paper) had civil and political equality. However, racial prejudice in the North continued and the bulk of the black population remained trapped in urban poverty. In some respects, the most surprising thing about the Northern black population after 1865 is that it did not suddenly increase as a result of a great exodus of Southern blacks north - a fear of many whites throughout the Civil War. This did not happen for two main reasons: most Southern blacks were too poor to move; and those who did move found it difficult to get jobs in the North.

c) Immigrants

The first two years of the Civil War had resulted in fewer immigrants being attracted to the USA. From 1863, however, immigration figures were back to their pre-war levels. Immigration trends in the twelve years after 1865 were similar to those in the twelve years before the Civil War. The great majority of the 3 million immigrants who settled in the USA in the 1860s and 1870s were of British, Irish, German and Scandinavian stock. (Not until the 1880s did immigrants from Southern and Eastern Europe begin to move en masse to the USA.) Immigrants tended to work, worship, socialise and marry largely within their own cultural groups. After 1865 there was a revival of the nativism that had been prevalent in the North throughout the 1850s. Irish Catholic immigrants were particularly unpopular. Some moves were made to restrict immigrants but they had mixed success. In 1875 a new law refused entry to prostitutes and to convicts whose sentences had been remitted in other countries on condition they leave.

Chinese immigrants, encouraged to come to the USA (and particularly to California) in the late 1860s to provide cheap labour to help build the Central Pacific Railroad, were even more unpopular than Irish Catholics. Once the transcontinental railroad was completed and Chinese workers began to compete with white Californians, resentment increased. By the early 1870s there were some 75,000 Chinese in California - about one ninth of the population. In the depression-hit years after 1873, most white Californians resented the fact that the Chinese often laboured for low wages and there were increasing demands to limit Chinese immigration. The 1877 Great Railroad Strike was to indirectly give rise to an anti-Chinese political movement. A San Francisco meeting, called to express sympathy for the strikers, ended with attacks on some passing Chinese. Within a few days sporadic anti-Chinese riots culminated in a mob attack on Chinatown. Within weeks a political movement arose, demanding an end to Chinese immigration. Although this movement quickly collapsed, the anti-Chinese theme became a national issue and in 1882 Congress voted to prohibit Chinese immigration.

10 Education

Industrialisation and urbanisation had a profound effect on all aspects of American life, including education. Indeed, the twelve years after the Civil War saw unprecedented advances in mass education and in every field of scholarship.

The crusade for universal public education had begun well before the Civil War. By 1861, most Northern states had public school systems and some 75 per cent of the North's children were receiving some formal education. But most attended school for only three or four years and few went to high school. There was concern that Americans lacked sufficient knowledge to participate wisely in public affairs or to function effectively as a labour force. After 1865, given that commitment to public education was well nigh universal, there was improvement and expansion at all levels. Before 1870 the only states with compulsory elementary school attendance were Massachusetts and Vermont but soon all Northern states had fallen into line. There was also an increase in secondary schools. By 1880 North Americans, as a whole, were as well educated as any people on earth. There was still room for improvement, especially in rural schools. Many teachers were poorly trained and often knew little more than their older pupils. Although American society revered education, it had little regard for teachers and paid them abysmally. An increasing number were women. There were also religious problems. Catholic immigrants, objecting to what they perceived to be the Protestant orientation of the public schools, often set up separate parochial school systems. In response, Republican politicians, resentful of Catholic immigrants' overwhelming preference for the Democrat Party, tried unsuccessfully in 1875 to pass a constitutional amendment cutting off all public aid to church-related schools. The Catholics in turn denounced federal aid to public schools as intending 'to suppress Catholic education, gradually extinguishing Catholicity in this country, and to form one homogeneous American people after the New England Evangelical type'.

After the Civil War, there was increased emphasis on higher education. Before 1861 most colleges were small, concerned mainly with training clergymen, and stifled by hidebound church leadership. Heavily classical oriented, they had poor libraries, laboratories and scientific apparatus. The USA had few scholars of real intellectual stature. The Morrill Act, passed in 1862, had an important impact on higher education. It granted each state warrants for 30,000 acres per Congressman, the income from which was to be applied to teaching agriculture and the mechanic arts. Among the first crop of newly-established land-grant colleges were the Universities of Illinois (1867), Minnesota (1868) and California (1868). All had a vocational emphasis but this did not mean they neglected academic subjects. By bringing higher education to hundreds of farm boys and girls, the agricultural colleges played an important role in training many of the USA's future scientists, teachers and community leaders. (Ironically, the colleges did not really meet the actual needs of farmers!) Other new Universities, e.g. Cornell (1868) and John Hopkins (1876), were the product of private philanthropy. Many of the new institutions encouraged new teaching methods and adopted new courses. Women's access to higher education improved markedly. All the Western state Universities were co-educational from the start and the performance of such women's colleges as Vassar (1865) and Wellesley (1875) refuted the common prejudice that women were academically less able than men.

By 1880 the USA had some 15 to 20 seats of learning which ranked with the best European universities. In every branch of learning American academics had begun to acquire international reputations. There was also growing emphasis on 'professionalism', with its imposition of standards, licensing of practitioners and accreditation of professional schools in fields such as law, medicine, pharmacy and dentistry. At Harvard in 1870 it was possible to qualify for a medical degree by attending two lecture courses for four months, proving three years of medical experience, and passing a simple examination. By 1880 the University insisted on three years of class attendance, together with laboratory and clinical work.

It has often been claimed that the decades following the Civil War were characterised by a materialism and a vulgarity that was hostile to intellectual and cultural activity. Certainly Americans produced little of value in music and drama and continued to look to Europe for inspiration in painting, sculpture and architecture. Nevertheless, the growth of cities provided a favourable environment for artistic and intellectual expression. There was an increasing interest in art and most large cities had galleries with sizeable collections. The so-called gilded age was also a creative period - and something of a watershed - in American literature as writers like Mark Twain developed a style of literary realism. Technical advance revolutionised the communication of ideas as dramatically as it transformed the transportation of goods or steel manufacture. Newspaper, magazine and book sales continued to rise as prices fell, with the result that most Americans were increasingly better informed.

11 Religion

Organised religion maintained its hold after 1865. Churches were usually crowded and the influence of the clergy was still substantial. Prominent preachers had national reputations and religious books and periodicals had large sales. But Protestantism, long the dominant force, faced grave challenges. Belief in the literal truth of the Bible was being undermined by the Darwinian theory of evolution. Industrialisation was posing questions which were difficult to answer within the framework of individual salvation, the traditional foundation of Protestant theology. There was also the threat from Catholicism, particularly in the cities.

Churchmen were slow to adjust to the needs of an industrialising society. Far from finding fault with the existing economic order, most Protestant clergymen provided theological justification for it. Membership of Protestant churches was becoming increasingly middle-class. Even denominations like the Baptists and Methodists had grown rich and respectable. (Rockefeller was a devout member of - and a generous benefactor to - the Baptist church.) Something of a gulf thus developed between the Protestant churches and the urban masses who rarely attended Protestant churches. Middle-class Protestants often showed little interest in providing aid or charity to the poor. Catholic leaders, committed to the idea that sin and vice were personal and that poverty was an act of God, also did little to help relieve poverty.

In the mid-1870s there was a resurgence of revivalism. Its foremost exponent was Dwight Moody, a former shoe salesman from Boston who became active in city missionary work after moving to Chicago in the 1850s. Moody had little formal education, was never ordained, and lacked the support of any ecclesiastical organisation, But he was successful in preaching a message of hope and reassurance. His sermons largely ignored the social issues. What concerned him was personal conversion, to be achieved through devout acceptance of the Bible. Moody's vivid preaching was accompanied and reinforced by Ira Sankey's gospel singing which had a powerful effect on congregations. Conducting campaigns in all the great American cities, they reached millions with their message. But as Moody himself acknowledged, their chief work was not to convert the unchurched masses but to strengthen and rekindle the faith of backsliders.

12 Conclusion

It is possible to exaggerate the social and economic changes which occurred in the North in the two decades after 1865. In 1880 most Northerners still lived on farms or in small villages or towns, not in large cities. Most industrial workers still worked in small factories and locally run businesses. Nevertheless, after 1865 the North had rapidly industrialised and by 1880 the USA was heading for world economic supremacy. In almost every aspect of economic life, there was increased productivity and intense competition. The most efficient companies - and often the most unscrupulous - survived, destroying or absorbing their foes. American industry was increasingly dominated by small groups of giant companies. Before 1880 little was done by federal or state governments to prevent consolidation and the threat of monopoly.

The social and economic changes were of considerable importance. However, arguably the Civil War had limited impact on the industrialisation process. The notion that the Civil War came about because of Northern industrial interests and that those same - triumphant - forces went on to control the USA in their best interest is far too simplistic. Northern business was no single monolithic interest engaged in a giant conspiracy to exploit the sectional crisis for its own ends. Instead it contained a variety of conflicting - and bitterly competitive - interests which disagreed with each other over many basic issues. If the manufacturing interests proved to be the chief economic beneficiaries of the war, this victory was an incidental rather than a planned result of the conflict. Although the powers of the national government had grown massively during the war, most of those powers did not long survive the coming of peace. Most Northern industrialists, like most Republican and Democrat politicians, were devoted to laissez-faire theories. Only with regard to tariffs was there support for government action. Most Americans - Northerners and Southerners, Republicans and Democrats alike - agreed on the need of tariffs: the question was simply how high they should be.

The Civil War did play a role in the North's economic and social development. In the short term, the war, if anything, may have inhibited rather than encouraged the North's economic growth. In the long term, the new financial system which emerged probably helped promote large-scale industrial enterprise. The war possibly gave a stimulus to new methods of production, organisation and marketing. It may have encouraged business leaders to think 'big'. It may well have brought about a redistribution of income in favour of North-eastern manufacturing interests. But, in general, the war's effect was to reaffirm and strengthen existing tendencies in Northern life rather than to transform them. In 1860 the USA was already the second greatest industrial nation on earth. Given Western expansion in the two decades after 1860, it is almost certain that industrial expansion would have occurred whether or not there had been a Civil War and whichever political party was in power thereafter. It is impossible to claim, therefore, that the war, in itself, brought about an economic and social revolution in the North.

Making notes on *'The Northern Economy and Society, 1865-77'*

Your notes on this chapter should give you an understanding of the process of industrialisation in the Northern states after 1865 and the economic and social effects of that process. As you read the chapter try to identify the contribution that the Civil War made to Northern industrialisation. It is my contention that most of the changes that occurred after 1865 were likely to have occurred whether or not there had been a Civil War. Do I provide enough evidence to support this contention? Do remember that many historians (like many American commentators in the 1860s and 1870s) have seen the Civil War as having a massive impact on Northern developments. What evidence would they have stressed in challenging the main thesis of this chapter?

Answering essay questions on *'The Northern Economy and Society, 1865-77'*

This chapter has focused on Northern economic and social developments after 1865. It is likely that questions on industrialisation will deal with national developments. This means you might well need to include paragraphs on developments in the South (see chapters 2 and 3) and West (see chapter 6). But do not panic! Most of the information you will need on industrialisation (and its results) will be found in this chapter. Consider the following questions:

1   Examine the main causes and results of the expansion of industrialisation in the USA in the two decades after 1865.
2   What impact did the Civil War have on the Northern economy and society?
3   Assess the impact that industrialisation had on American life in the two decades after 1865.
4   To what extent did the changes occurring in American economic and social life after 1865 amount to 'a second American revolution'?

Re-arrange the questions in order of difficulty. Which do you think is the easiest and which the most difficult? Many students will identify question 3 as the easiest because on the surface, it can be answered in a straightforward, descriptive manner. It is because such questions can be answered simply - at a low level - that they are dangerous. It is easy - but wrong - to write a narrative answer writing everything you know about industrialisation. There are two key words in the question. One is 'Assess': this means you are being asked to make judgements about the impact of industrialisation. The other is 'American': this means you must examine national - not just Northern - developments. The question has suddenly become much harder! Brainstorm the kinds of information you would be including in the answer and how you might consider organising the material. The summary diagram on page 93 should help provide a rough plan for question 1, so let us move straight on to questions 2 and 4. The subject matter for both these questions is similar but will obviously need to be organised differently in order to answer the specific questions. Try drawing up a rough plan for either question 2 or question 4. Assume you will be writing an essay of about 7 or 8 paragraphs. What would they contain? Now write an introduction and conclusion, both of 7 or 8 sentences in length. Imagine an examiner only reads the introduction and conclusion. Does your introduction set the scene? Does your conclusion present a good summary of the rest of the planned essay? Do your introduction and conclusion together go a long way to answering the set question? If not, think of ways you could improve matters. If so, remember to use the successful formula in future essays!

Source-based questions on 'The Northern Economy and Society, 1865-77'

1 The McCormick Factory and Reaper
Examine the illustrations on page 69 and 75. Answer the following questions:
a) Why does the factory seem well sited? (2 marks)
b) How might the people of North Side Chicago have regarded the McCormick factory in 1869? (5 marks)
c) What do the two sources tell us about the state of American manufacturing industry in 1869? (8 marks)

2 Entrepreneurs
Read the extracts from Rockefeller, Carnegie and Vanderbilt on page 78 and 79. Answer the following questions:
a) How do the three sources help explain the success of the great entrepreneurs? (7 marks)
b) What do the sources not tell us about how entrepreneurs achieved their success? (8 marks)

3 Sewing Machine Production
Examine the sewing machine statistics on page 76. Answer the following questions:
a) What do the statistics suggest about economic booms and slumps in the USA after 1865? (5 marks)
b) Which sources might historians have to consult to help explain why Singer was more successful than the other two companies? (5 marks)
c) What impact might the increased sales of sewing machines have had on American life? (5 marks)

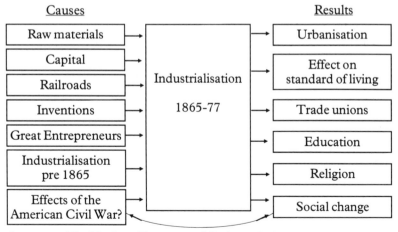

Summary - The Northern Economy and Society, 1865-77

CHAPTER 5

Northern Political Developments, 1865-77

1 Introduction

The Civil War left Northerners in control of United States politics. The Republican Party - the most popular Northern party - was to be the dominant party in the USA down to the 1930s. Northerners also tended to dominate the Democrat Party. Although the power base of the Democrat Party was in the South, Democrat presidential candidates came mainly from the North. Only by winning substantial Northern support could the Democrats hope to win a national election. The Northern dominance of American politics was one of the results of the Civil War. Whether it was an important result is a subject of some debate. It should have enhanced the power of the North to enact federal legislation beneficial to its interests. However, it is far from clear that this was the case. Northerners, in fact, had a variety of - often conflicting - concerns. It has also been claimed that most politicians in the decades following the Civil War were only concerned about their own - selfish - interests. In 1873 Mark Twain and Charles Dudley Warner collaborated on a novel entitled *The Gilded Age*. The novel's title has become an enduring tag for the politics of the time. Twain's aim was to satirize two aspects of contemporary American life: the pervading 'speculativeness' and materialism of the times; and 'the shameful corruption' which Twain noted had 'lately crept into our politics'. Henry Adams, an acerbic commentator of political developments of the late nineteenth century, saw the two decades after 1865 as 'poor in purpose and barren in achievement'. Most historians have also been critical of the politics and politicians of the period (especially the years 1869 to 1877 when Ulysses S. Grant was President), seeing it as an age of jobbery, profiteering and false glitter.

Yet many contemporaries saw the age as truly golden - not gilded. They viewed its materialism as productive, not exploitive. Certainly America remained the most democratic nation on earth and most historians accept that the politicians generally expressed the people's will. Most politicians, far from being corrupt self-seekers, were men of great vigour, imagination and patriotism: many had fought bravely - sometimes heroically - for principle and high idealism in the Civil War. Moreover, this was a period when, in many ways, the USA was remarkably successful. Certainly the potential power of the nation was increasing. By 1880 the USA was on the verge of replacing Britain as the greatest industrial and manufacturing power in the world. Did this happen in spite of - or because of - politicians?

This chapter then has two main concerns. To what extent were

American politics effected by the Civil War? How bad were the politics and politicians of the Gilded Age?

2 Federal Government

Before the outbreak of Civil War, the federal government had relatively little power. Most functions of government were handled at state and local level. The local postmaster apart, it was rare for Americans to encounter an official representative of national authority. However, the exigencies of war resulted in the federal government having a greatly expanded income, bureaucracy and set of responsibilities. During the war, the federal government was forced to introduce conscription and train, equip and co-ordinate the activities of millions of men. The federal budget, amounting to $63 million in 1860, had risen to well over $1 billion by 1865. At the war's end the federal bureaucracy, with 53,000 employees, was the largest employer in the nation. Radical Republicans, in particular, extolled the increased power of the federal government, regarding it as one of the most salutory of the war's consequences. 'The policy of this country', declared Senator John Sherman (brother of General Sherman), 'ought to be to make everything national as far as possible; to nationalise our country so that we shall love our country'. For many radicals, the nation had become the custodian of freedom. Freedom, they were convinced, stood in greater danger of abridgement from local than national authority. After 1865 some questioned whether the states should continue to wield any meaningful power.

Certainly the outcome of the war shifted the balance of the federal system in a national direction and strengthened the federal government in Washington. However, this is not to say that there was a revolution in the way that the USA was governed. So many of the functions assumed by government during the war were clearly exceptional and justified only by unique circumstances. With the end of hostilities, the federal government quickly disbanded its armed forces, reduced its bureaucracy, abdicated some of its economic management responsibilities, and tried to return to its old modest scale. The war had weakened but not destroyed the idea of state rights. Although Northerners had been prepared to fight a bloody Civil War to ensure that individual states did not have the right to secede from the Union, most Republicans accepted local control over local issues and had no wish to do away with state governments. In the years after 1865 state governments were greatly to expand their responsibilities for issues such as public health, welfare and education.

3 The Political Parties

The two main political parties remained the Republicans and the Democrats. Although Americans were remarkably loyal to one or the other party, many historians regard the two parties as being essentially the same. Lord Bryce, a perceptive British observer of the American political scene, wrote in the 1880s;

1 Neither party has any principles, any distinctive tenets. Both have traditions. Both claim to have tendencies. Both have certain war cries, organisations, interests enlisted in their support. But those interests are in the main the interests of getting or keeping the
5 patronage of government. Tenets and policies, points of political doctrine and points of political practice, have all but vanished... All has been lost, except office or the hope of it.

In 1879 Woodrow Wilson, a future President but then a young College graduate, said much the same when he described the American political system as: 'No leaders, no principles; no principles, no parties'. Wilson believed that both Democrat and Republican politicians ignored or fudged the main issues of the day - issues that grew out of intense social and economic change. Like many observers at the time and since, Wilson thought that politicians were concerned simply with obtaining and holding office - and benefiting financially from so doing. The late nineteenth century was the heyday of the political machine and the 'spoils system'. Parties vied for control of federal and state patronage (in the form of government jobs and contracts). Historians have often claimed that real political control lay with party bosses who controlled local party 'machines'. Democrat city bosses were stereotyped as men of little education and usually of Irish stock. Republican state bosses, by contrast, tended to be well-educated, and of old-American stock: many were US Senators. The power of the bosses rested on control of federal and/or state patronage.

It is difficult to generalise about the two main parties. Each was a collection of state and local organisations. They temporarily assumed a national character once every four years during presidential elections. At other times they nominated candidates, raised funds, conducted campaigns, distributed patronage, and were largely independent. Both parties, at state and federal level, were plagued by chronic factionalism, the product of personal rivalries and the lure of spoils. In both Houses of Congress there were continually shifting alliances. However, most Republicans - and most Democrats -did have certain things in common. Both parties support rested to a large extent on historical, ethnic, religious and cultural factors. Moreover, it is - and was - possible to discern real and persistent differences of emphasis on questions of public policy.

The Republicans, though accepting local control over local issues, believed that an integrated economy and a nationwide society implied active centralised government. They stood for a high protective tariff, supported - or at least paid lip service to - the notion of racial equality, and often sympathised with, without actually endorsing, prohibition, Sabbatarianism and immigration restriction. Above all, the Republican Party saw itself as the party of Union. Civil War memories were the cement that bound the party together. In election after election, Republican candidates invoked Lincoln's name and identified the Democrats with harbouring notions of disunion. The Republicans were strongest in New England and the states of the upper Midwest. They drew support predominantly from non-Southern, small town, native-born Protestants. Most of the business community, many skilled industrial workers, large numbers of better-off Northern farmers, and the vast majority of African Americans voted Republican. The party could also count on the support of men who had fought for the Union in the Civil War. Veterans organisations, like the Grand Army of the Republic, founded in 1866, were not merely social clubs, welfare organisations and outlets for those who wished to remember the excitement of their youth: they were also powerful political pressure groups.

The Democrat Party in the North emerged from the Civil War remarkably intact despite the defections of a number of prominent War Democrats and an internal division between those who supported the war effort, while criticising specific administration policies, and those who advocated immediate peace. While it could count upon massive support from whites in ex-Confederate states, it could also rely on the support of many Midwestern farmers, some of whom had close ties with the South. More important, it had the support of most Irish and German Catholic immigrants. To unite these groups, the Democrats built upon an ideological appeal which identified the Republican Party as an agent of economic privilege and political centralisation and a threat to individual liberty and the tradition of limited government. The Democrat Party remained the party of state rights and small government. The Republican economic policies, Democrats claimed, enriched North-eastern capitalists at the expense of ordinary farmers and labourers. Democrats opposed high protective tariffs, and state and federal aid to private corporations. Most were also hostile to the Republican perfectionist reform tradition - especially prohibition and Sabbatarianism. The potent cry of white supremacy provided the final ideological glue in the Democrat coalition. Once the Southern states returned to full participation in national politics in the 1870s, the Democrats were able to mount a serious challenge to the essentially Northern Republican Party.

However, although there were fundamental differences of principle (and tradition) between the Republicans and the Democrats, on many national issues of the day the two parties pursued policies of evasion. On questions of the currency, regulation of big business, farm problems, civil service reform, internal improvements and immigration it is - and was - hard to distinguish between the parties and there was often fierce divisions within parties. As presidential election day approached, parties tried (with varying degrees of success) to patch up their squabbles and present a facade of unity. This seemed essential because both parties were remarkably even. National elections tended to depend on state party organisations in the 'swing' states - New York, New Jersey, Indiana and Illinois. For much of the late nineteenth century, the main parties were so closely balanced, they often hesitated to take clear positions on controversial questions lest by so doing they divided their party and lost potential support. There was nothing very unusual about this. Major American parties have often avoided clear-cut standing on controversial questions in order to appeal to as wide a segment of the electorate as possible.

There is no doubt that corruption was a feature of politics at every level in the decades after the Civil War. It is most associated with the presidency of Grant. (Indeed the term 'Grantism' was soon in common usage as a shorthand reference of unbridled corruption.) Certainly the level of political morality was often abysmal. Names of people long dead were solemnly inscribed in voting registers, their suffrage rights exercised by imposters. Politicians continued to manipulate the spoils system to reward party workers. They also tried to ensure that state or national government furthered or defended the interests of a particular place or region. But corruption went beyond this. Each party had its share of corrupt officials, willing to buy and sell government appointments or congressional votes. Each had men who were in the pay of big business - especially railroad companies which gave a host of favours to politicians, editors and other leaders in positions to influence public opinion. Much of the corruption stemmed from state and federal government's policies of promoting railroad development and granting land and millions of dollars in direct aid to support railroad construction. This resulted in railroad companies 'buying' politicians. (The Pennsylvania state legislature was described as the finest body of men that money could buy.) New scandals were exposed at all levels of politics in the late 1860s and early 1870s as money was funnelled into the pockets both of individuals and political parties.

Dishonest and incompetent officials were particularly prevalent at city level. The breakneck speed at which cities grew was a major factor. With large-scale expansion of public utilities (such as gas and water), corrupt alliances developed between unscrupulous city officials and business interests, eager for franchises and contracts. The most notorious example of municipal corruption was the 'Tweed Ring', led by William Tweed, in New York. Between 1869 and 1871 Tweed's Democrat machine dispensed 60,000 patronage positions and increased the city's debt by $70 million through graft and inflated contracts. Indeed, Tweed and his accomplices may have siphoned off as much as $200 million from New York over a ten year period. The scale of the corruption was beyond anything seen in the South. By 1871, the Tweed Ring's misdeeds had become so flagrant that it provoked a reaction. Helped by newspaper exposés, a reform coalition, led by wealthy lawyer Samuel Tilden, finally broke Tweed's power and sent him to jail on charges of fraud and extortion. His successor, 'Honest' John Kelly, while hardly meriting his nickname, at least gave New York a respite from the grosser forms of wrong-doing.

Not all Americans were concerned by the corruption. They accepted it as a political fact of life. Moreover, city bosses often helped provide welfare, especially for immigrant groups, who repaid their benefactors with their votes. Although Tweed defrauded New York of millions of dollars, he remained popular among many Irish voters, largely because his massive stealing provided him with the funds for an elaborate welfare system, enabling him to give substantial aid to Catholic schools and the large-scale distribution of food and fuel to the poor. Not all political bosses - and by no means all politicians - were crooked. Nor were all the alliances of business and politics corrupt. Many politicians favoured particular business interests out of conviction. Others received favours (for example, free passes from railroad companies) but felt no obligation to the companies that handed them out.

Though politics may have seemed corrupt and dull to disillusioned patricians like Henry Adams, it did not seem so to ordinary Americans. Indeed, the period after the Civil War was an age of fierce political partisanship and exciting campaigns. Voter turnout remained remarkably high - often over 80 per cent - and large numbers of people attended political gatherings. Voters - and politicians - thought far more was at stake in elections than spoils. They believed they were dealing with real issues. In many respects they were right. The tariff, currency reform, civil service reform, Southern reconstruction and immigration were all vital issues which divided Americans. At local level, issues such as temperance and Sunday observance, were often similarly important and divisive.

4 The Presidency of Andrew Johnson

Johnson's presidency was mainly concerned with the issue of Southern reconstruction. (This has been dealt with in chapter 2.) By 1867 the President was clearly at odds with most Northern Congressmen and came very close to being impeached in 1868. In the last two years of his presidency, Johnson was very much a lame duck. Although the impeachment of Johnson failed, it helped shift the balance of power in the direction of Congress.

However, Johnson's presidency was not an entire failure. His

Secretary of State, William Seward, had some success. During the Civil War, Napoleon III of France had established a protectorate over Mexico, setting up Archduke Maximilian of Austria as emperor. The United States had long opposed all intervention on the American continent. But Abraham Lincoln, not wishing to fight two wars at the same time, had done little more than express diplomatic disapproval at France's action. Once the Civil War ended, Seward demanded that the French withdraw their forces and moved 50,000 American troops to the Rio Grande in 1866 to reinforce his threat. In 1866-7 Napoleon III did pull his troops out of Mexico and nationalist Mexican rebels promptly seized and executed Maximilian. Fear of American intervention had been only one of several reasons prompting Napoleon's decision. But it was a reason. After 1865 no European country (not even Britain) felt strong enough to challenge the USA on the North American continent which was perceived to be the USA's own 'backyard'.

Seward rid North America of another foreign power when in 1867 he succeeded in purchasing Alaska from Russia at a cost of a mere $7.2 million. This was Seward's greatest achievement. Determined to assist United States commerce with the Far East, Seward also acquired Midway Island in the West Pacific in 1867 and made some overtures towards annexing Hawaii. But Seward's expansionist ambitions in the Caribbean, fueled by American business interests, were frustrated by Congress. Efforts to win land in Santo Domingo in 1865 came to nothing. In July 1867 Seward signed a treaty with Denmark to purchase the Virgin Islands for $7.5 million. The treaty crashed because the Senate opposed spending more on a few small islands than it had spent on purchasing Alaska.

5 The 1868 Presidential Election

The Republicans had many advantages in 1868. The party controlled a great deal of patronage: it had the power to admit or exclude whichever Southern states it saw fit; and, given its control of Congress, it had the opportunity to shape legislation with an eye to votes. It also had the emotional appeal of being the party that had conducted the administration during the Civil War. In the North the Democrats had to live down as best they could the accusation of alleged 'disloyalty' during the War. The Democrats also suffered from the discrediting of Andrew Johnson, with whose policies they were associated. Nevertheless, the Democrats had done well in the 1867 state elections and Republican leaders were aware they needed a strong candidate in 1868 around whom the party and the North could unite.

The Republicans found it easy to agree on that candidate: the great war hero General Ulysses S. Grant. Although Grant had usually voted Democrat before the war, it was clear by the late 1860s that he was a committed Republican. It was also clear that he had presidential ambitions. At first he had tried to remain neutral as Johnson and the Republican leaders fell out but by 1868 he had committed himself to the anti-Johnson forces. At the Republican convention in Chicago in May, Grant was unanimously nominated on the first ballot. Although he lacked political experience and had never before stood for any political office, he seemed an excellent candidate. As overall leader of the Union army from 1864, he had displayed considerable political skills. The fact that he had served in Johnson's cabinet, ensured that he had at least some awareness of the way that government in Washington operated. Professional politicians were confident that he would follow the advice of Republican Congressional leaders.

The Republican platform endorsed the reconstruction policy of Congress. One plank cautiously defended black suffrage as a necessity in the South, but a matter each Northern state should settle for itself. Another urged payment of the national debt 'in the utmost good faith to all creditors': this meant in gold. Grant, himself, seems to have felt strongly about few issues. His main slogan throughout the campaign was: 'Let us have peace'. Democrats took opposite positions on both reconstruction and the debt. The Republican Congress, the Democrat platform charged, instead of restoring the Union had 'subjected ten states, in the time of profound peace, to military despotism and Negro supremacy'. Democrats denounced radical reconstruction as revolutionary and called for state regulation of the suffrage question. As to the public debt, the party endorsed the view that since most bonds had been bought with depreciated greenbacks, they should be paid off in greenbacks, not gold (unless they actually specified payment in gold). The Democrat convention chose Horatio Seymour, war governor of New York, as the party's presidential candidate.

The Republican campaign consisted mainly of 'waving the bloody shirt' - emphasising their war record and reviling the Democrats for their alleged disloyalty. The Democrats, in contrast, damned Grant as a 'Black Republican and as a 'nigger lover'. In the event Grant won 26 of the 34 states and swept the electoral college by 214 to 80 votes. But the Democrats actually made a closer race of it than the electoral college vote implies. Grant's popular majority was only 307,000 out of a total of over 5.7 million votes. Without the 600,000 black votes cast for him in the seven reconstructed states, Grant would have been a minority president.

6 Grant's First Term

Grant brought to the presidency less political experience than any man who had ever occupied the office, except perhaps Zachary Taylor - another soldier. His political naivety was evident in his choice of advisers. He took little account of party or popular feeling, instead handing round appointments to men he found congenial. Of the 25 men he appointed to his cabinet during his 8 years in the White House, most were undistinguished and several were rascals. As time went on he displayed an unfortunate gift for losing men of talent and integrity from his cabinet. Grant's lack of judgement was also revealed in his acceptance of gifts from favour-seekers such as the financier Jay Cooke. Although Grant was personally honest, his fondness for shoddy company and his misplaced loyalty to associates who were incompetent or dishonest or both helped depress standards of political morality. In general, he took a narrow view of the presidential office, regarding it as largely ceremonial and symbolic. He conceived that it was his duty to carry out the laws. In the formulation of policy he tended passively to follow the lead of Congress. This approach endeared him at first to party leaders, but it left him at last ineffective.

Financial issues dominated the political agenda during Grant's presidency. In order to meet the financial demands of the Civil War, the federal government had issued its own paper currency - known as greenbacks. After the war the Treasury had assumed that the $400 million worth of greenbacks issued during the conflict would be withdrawn from circulation and that the nation would revert to a 'hard-money' currency (i.e. gold and silver coin). Many agrarian and debtor groups resisted this contraction of the money supply, believing that it would mean lower prices for their crops and that it would make it harder for them to pay long-term debts. Others thought that inflation would generate more rapid economic growth. In 1868 congressional supporters of such a 'soft-money' policy halted the retirement of greenbacks, leaving $356 million outstanding. This was the situation when Grant took office.

The Republicans, aware that there was a deeply ingrained popular assumption that hard money was morally preferable to paper currency, had fought the election campaigning for hard money. In his inaugural address in March 1869 Grant endorsed payment of the national debt in gold as a point of national honour.

1 A great debt has been contracted in securing to us and our posterity the Union. The payment of this, principal and interest, as well as the return to a specie basis as soon as it can be accomplished without material detriment to the debtor class or to the country at
5 large, must be provided for. To protect the national honour, every dollar of Government indebtedness should be paid in gold, unless otherwise expressly stipulated in the contract. Let it be understood that no repudiator of one farthing of our public debt will be trusted in public place, and it will go far toward strengthening a credit
10 which ought to be the best in the world, and will ultimately enable us to replace the debt with bonds bearing less interest than we now pay. To this should be added a faithful collection of the revenue, a strict accountability to the Treasury for every dollar collected, and

the greatest practicable retrenchment in expenditure in every
15 department of Government. When we compare the paying
capacity of the country now, with the ten States in poverty from the
effects of war, but soon to emerge, I trust, into greater prosperity
than ever before, with its paying capacity twenty five years ago, and
20 calculate what it probably will be twenty-five years hence, who can
doubt the feasibility of paying every dollar then with more ease
than we now pay for useless luxuries? Why it looks as though
Providence had bestowed upon us a strong box in the precious
metals locked up in the sterile mountains of the far West, and
25 which we are now forging the key to unlock, to meet the very
contingency that is now upon us

In March 1869 the Public Credit Act, which endorsed the principle that
outstanding debt should be paid in gold, became the first act of
Congress Grant signed. This enriched those who had bought Treasury
bonds with depreciated greenbacks.

The complexities of the 'money questions' exasperated Grant. The
President was often troubled with personal money matters and making
national monetary policy did not come any easier. His administration
was soon troubled by financial scandal. This first touched Grant in the
summer of 1869 when the crafty banker Jay Gould and the flamboyant
James 'Jubilee Jim' Fisk connived to corner the national market in gold.
They aimed to buy as much gold as they could on the New York Stock
Exchange until they owned a major part of the USA's supply. They
would then refuse to sell it. The resulting shortage should drive up the
price of gold, ensuring that when the two men finally sold the precious
metal, they would make a fabulous profit. To succeed, their operation
required the co-operation of the US Treasury which owned over
$80,000,000 of gold. The Treasury could sell enough gold at any time to
hold down the price and wreck the plan. Gould and Fisk employed
Grant's brother-in-law to extract a vague presidential assurance that the
Treasury intended to halt gold supplies. As the rumour spread on Wall
Street that Grant intended to refrain from selling gold on the market, the
gold price soared to $163 an ounce. Grant belatedly realised what was
afoot and authorised release of sufficient gold to foil the plot. The gold
bubble burst. In a crazy 15 minutes the price of gold fell to only $30 an
ounce. Many speculators - though not Gould or Fisk - suffered great
losses. Grant was severely criticised for his gullibility.

It seemed to many that Grant's administration worked closely with -
and on behalf of - business interests. By 1870 Congress had repealed all
wartime excise duties except those on drink and tobacco. In 1872 it
abolished the wartime income tax. However, Congress, with industrialist backing, successfully resisted all attempts to lower the high tariffs
imposed during the war, ostensibly as emergency revenue measures.
Some of the rates were increased. Money seemed to 'talk'. In the early

1870s a number of scandals - most of them involving graft, bribery and corrupt financial dealings - attracted the public's attention. Some involved members of Grant's inner circle. Others involved city bosses. (The exposure of the Tweed Ring in 1871 revealed the amazing extent to which corruption could go in New York.)

Increasingly some reform-minded Republicans became disgruntled with corruption in government (at whatever level) in general and with Grant's administration, in particular. They began to campaign for the creation of a professional civil service, staffed by well-educated men who were appointed on merit and who had permanent tenure. This, the reformers argued, would raise the administrative efficiency of American government, essential as government took on an expanding role, and the number of federal and state employees increased. It would also reduce corruption. They pressed their ideas on Grant and the nation with an almost religious fervour. But Grant was aware that many Republican politicians opposed civil service reform. The counter-reform argument stressed that patronage was the lifeblood of politics and that parties could not function without armies of loyal political workers who expected and deserved the rewards of office - if they won. Moreover, a competitive examination system for entry to the civil service would ensure that only well-educated (and thus by and large wealthy) men would have much opportunity of gaining office. This was seen as a threat to the - democratic - American way. There was a danger of establishing an aristocracy of office-holders, insulated from the will of the people.

Grant momentarily heartened the reformers in 1871 by persuading Congress to establish a Civil Service Commission, authorised to devise a merit system, similar to that in Britain, for federal employees. But under pressure from spoilsmen he gave only minimal support to the new agency and it finally expired through lack of funds. Grant's half-hearted support of civil service reform disappointed the reformers. Equally offensive to reformers was Grant's dismissal of Attorney General Ebenezer Hoar and Secretary of the Interior Jacob Cox, regarded as the best men in his administration. Their departure meant that by 1870 virtually every cabinet officer of ability and integrity, with the exception of Secretary of State Hamilton Fish, had been ousted.

Grant's efforts to annex Santo Domingo (the present day Dominican Republic) also alienated the 'reforming' wing of his party. But Grant, who was personally committed to the scheme, knew that he could count on powerful support. He was aware that the US navy desired a Caribbean naval base and that American banking and business interests also favoured annexation. Many Americans believed it was the USA's 'manifest destiny' to rule all North America and the Caribbean. Others, like Grant himself, thought that the island might provide a suitable base for American blacks. Some ex-abolitionists, like Frederick Douglass, believed that annexation would benefit the - mainly black - population of the island. Interestingly, the ruling Santo Domingo political faction was also keen on annexation, hoping to save itself from overthrow in a continuing civil war.

In 1869 Grant, without informing Secretary of State Hamilton Fish, sent his former private secretary Orville Babcock to negotiate a treaty of annexation. The island's government quickly agreed to the American proposals. Little real effort was made to consult the people of the island. A plebiscite, held with only four days advance notice, was coupled with a warning that the opponents of the treaty would be executed. Not surprisingly, the plebiscite produced a resounding vote in favour of annexation. Grant sent the annexation treaty to the Senate. Realising that Charles Sumner, Chairman of the Senate's Foreign Relations Committee, was a key man, Grant made several efforts to woo him - to no effect. Sumner was implacably opposed to imperialism. He was also concerned about the African race. Grant's annexation treaty would threaten the independence of Santo Domingo's neighbour - Haiti, the hemisphere's only black republic. Sumner believed that the Haiti republic should be maintained as an example and an inspiration. Other Senators had no wish to take Santo Domingo because it would mean increasing the United States' non-white population. Some believed it would complicate US relations with European powers. Annexation would certainly involve the US in San Domingo's civil war. According to one Philadelphia newspaper, 'The True interests of the American people will be better served ... by a thorough and complete development of the immense resources of our existing territory than by any rash attempts to increase it'.

Although the majority of the Republican Senators supported annexation, it proved impossible to get the two thirds majority necessary for the treaty to be accepted. (In June 1871 a Senate vote on the treaty resulted in a 28-28 tie.) By this stage, relations between Grant and Sumner were at rock bottom and the Senator's attacks on Grant became increasingly personal and vindictive. In December 1871, at Grant's behest, Sumner was deprived of the Chair of the Senate Foreign Relations Committee. Grant never abandoned his commitment to annexation but renewed efforts to take over Santo Domingo also failed.

Grant's government had other concerns in the Caribbean. In 1868 Cuban rebels began a serious war to win independence from Spain. The Cuban rebels sought aid from the USA: some sought American annexation. Although Grant supported this notion in principle, Secretary of State Fish had no wish to take-over an island where there were so few 'pure' whites and where the population was not ready (in his view) to take on board the rights and responsibilities of American citizens. Instead Fish supported the principle of Cuban independence and hoped that American business interests might establish an 'unofficial' empire over the island. In this way the USA would effectively control the island without having day-to-day responsibilities. But Fish, while sympathising with the Cuban rebels, had no wish to get involved in a war with Spain. The United States, therefore, remained officially neutral. The revolt was to continue until 1878 when rebel internal divisions enabled Spain to re-establish an uneasy control.

Grant's administration had one major success in foreign policy. Since 1865 Britain and the USA had been at odds over whether Britain should pay compensation for the help it had given to the Confederacy during the Civil War. Some Senators claimed that British assistance had maintained the Confederacy for the last two years of the war and that in consequence Britain should foot the war bill - some $2 billion. Others (more realistically) thought Britain should at least pay compensation for the damage wrought by Confederate commerce raiders, like the 'Alabama', which had been built in British shipyards and then proceeded to extensively damage the North's merchant marine. US-British negotiations over this matter had dragged on and on. But in 1871-2 the differences were resolved. Britain agreed to pay $15.5 million in compensation for damage inflicted by the 'Alabama'. The Treaty of Washington, signed in September 1872, ended the possibility of a serious Anglo-American crisis.

7 The 1872 Election

Long before Grant's first term was over, opposition to his policies had led to mutiny within the Republican ranks. Many of the President's opponents were personally disaffected: they felt they had been pushed aside by Grant and his administration. Most were angry that the President had not committed the Republican Party to civil service reform. The controversy over the annexation of Santo Domingo alienated some. Others disliked Grant's support for tough reconstruction measures (e.g. the Force Acts against the Ku Klux Klan): they thought the time had come to wash their hands of the South and concentrate on more important economic matters. Most of Grant's Republican opponents held 'conservative' economic views: they favoured free trade, hard money, and less taxation. Many believed that reconstruction exemplified all the bad consequences of government action. Blacks should no longer be mollycoddled: they must learn to stand on their own feet. Men of 'intelligence and culture' should be restored to power - both in the North and in the South. (In the South this meant restoring white Southerners to office.)

By 1871 the dissidents were known collectively as Liberal Republicans. Their leaders included some distinguished figures: Carl Schurz, a German revolutionary who had been successively American diplomat, Civil War general, and Missouri Senator; Charles Francis Adams, American Minister to London during the Civil War; and Gideon Welles, Lincoln's Secretary of the Navy. While the movement attracted the support of a galaxy of influential newspaper editors, Liberal Republicanism lacked popular support. It was too much a movement of the 'great' and 'good'. The word 'reform', noted New York Democrat chief Horatio Seymour, 'is not popular with the workingmen. To them it means less money spent and less work'. Ordinary Americans preferred the unreformed spoils system that at least gave them a chance of attaining office. Another weakness of Liberal Republicanism was its heterogeneous character. Gathered under the same political umbrella were high protectionists, free traders, eastern conservatives, western radicals, idealistic reformers and practical politicians. The only unifying factor was dislike of Grant.

In May 1872 the Liberal Republicans held a national convention at Cincinnati. The convention, while not agreeing on tariff policy, condemned Grant's reconstruction policies, supported reconciliation with the South, proposed a resumption of specie payments on greenbacks, and supported civil service reform. The following extract was part of their platform.

1 The Civil Service of the Government has become a mere instrument of partisan tyranny and personal ambition, and an object of selfish greed. It is a scandal and reproach upon free institutions, and breeds a demoralization dangerous to the
5 perpetuity of republican government. We therefore regard such thorough reforms of the Civil Service as one of the most pressing necessities of the hour; that honesty, capacity, and fidelity constitute the only valid claims to public employment; that the offices of the Government cease to be a matter of arbitrary
10 favoritism and patronage, and that public station become again a post of honour. To this end it is imperatively required that no President shall be a candidate for re-election.

Horace Greeley, the editor of the *New York Tribune,* was nominated as the Liberal Republican presidential candidate. Greeley, who had a history of erratic judgement and supporting odd causes, was an unusual choice. He was opposed to free trade and had strongly opposed civil service reform. Liberal Republican leaders, involved in secret discussions with Democrat leaders in an effort to unite the parties and run one candidate against Grant, were aware that Greeley was not the perfect choice. Although he had advocated treating the South leniently since 1865, he had a reputation of being a bitter opponent of the Democrat Party and it seemed unlikely that he would attract many Democrat voters. Nevertheless, the Democrats gave their nomination to Greeley as the only hope of beating Grant.

Most Republicans drew ranks behind Grant. He claimed to be the man of the people. A national hero, he stood for order and peace, remained popular with ordinary Northerners, and could count on the support of most traditional Republican voters. Although there was corruption in Washington, Grant seemed apart from it. In contrast to

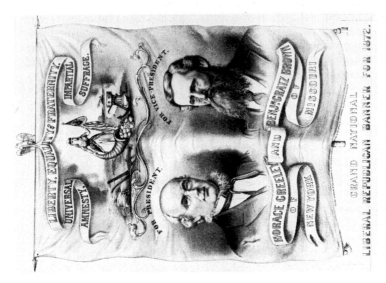

A Liberal Republican election poster, 1872

A Republican election poster, 1872

the venality of many politicians, he seemed all the purer. Greeley, despite an exhausting tour of the USA, won only three ex-Confederate states (Georgia, Texas and Tennessee), three border states (Kentucky, Maryland and Missouri) and not a single Northern state. Grant won over 55 per cent of the popular vote. The election was a personal tragedy for Greeley. Not only had he been humiliatingly defeated, but his wife had died during the campaign. Worn out with grief and fatigue, Greeley himself died three weeks after the election. Liberal Republicanism did not long survive him. Many of the leading Liberal Republicans, like Carl Schurz, eventually returned to the Republican fold.

8 Grant's Second Term

Grant's second term was far more difficult than his first. One political scandal followed another. The first major revelations concerned the Credit Mobilier, the construction company formed to build the Union Pacific railroad. Having made immense profits for a handful of large shareholders by charging well over twice the real construction costs, the directors (who controlled both the Union Pacific and the Credit Mobilier) had sought to avert a Congressional investigation by distributing stock at discount to influential Congressmen. All this had occurred before Grant took office but with many leading Republicans implicated, the President could not entirely escape the odium.

Subsequent exposures revealed that the administration, though not Grant personally, were deeply corrupt. During Grant's two terms, the Secretary of the Treasury, the Attorney General and the Secretary of the Interior were all forced to resign because of suspected or proven official misconduct. The Secretary of the Navy was shown to have been negligent - or worse - in awarding contracts. The Secretary of War was found to have taken bribes from aspirants to traderships on Indian reservations. Impeached by the House of Representatives, he escaped conviction only because Grant - 'with great regret' - accepted his hasty resignation.

Economic distress followed close upon the public scandals besetting Grant's administration. During 1873 the market for railroad bonds turned sour as some 25 companies defaulted on their interest payments. The firm of Jay Cooke and Company, a pillar of the USA's banking system, unable to sell the bonds of the Northern Pacific Railroad, went bankrupt in September 1873. More banks failed and the stock market had temporarily to suspend operations. The '1873 Panic' set off a six year depression, the longest and most severe that Americans had yet suffered, marked by widespread bankruptcies, rising unemployment and a drastic reduction in railroad building. By 1876 over half of the nation's railroads had defaulted on their banks and were in the hands of the receivers.

The panic focused attention once more on the status of greenbacks.

Radicals and debtors were now even more forceful in demanding that the government retain or increase the $356 million greenbacks already in circulation, believing that by increasing the money supply the country could spend its way out of depression. Conservatives and creditors, on the other hand, still preferred a policy of sound money and insisted that if greenbacks were to be retained, the government should stabilise their value by making them redeemable in gold. As a relief measure and in an effort to stimulate business, the Treasury reluctantly re-issued $26 million in greenbacks previously withdrawn. Similar considerations led Congress in 1874 to propose to raise the greenback total to $400 million. For a time the advocates of paper money seemed to be riding high. But Grant vetoed the 1874 bill to issue more greenbacks and in December 1874 called for redemption of greenbacks in gold. In January 1875, before the Republicans gave up control of the House, Congress passed the Resumption Act. This guaranteed payment in gold to people who turned in their paper money after 1 January 1879. This gave the Treasury time to build up a gold reserve for that purpose and was designed to reduce the greenbacks in circulation. This act infuriated those who wanted a 'soft' monetary policy and the 'money question' was destined to remain one of the most divisive issues in American politics.

The Republicans suffered a catastrophic defeat in the 1874 mid-term elections. Given the depression, voters turned against the party in power. In the greatest reversal of partisan alignment in the entire nineteenth century, the massive 110 vote Republican majority in the House was transformed into a Democrat majority of 60 seats. The Democrats also came close to winning control of the Senate. Congress was now all but paralysed. New departures in national policy became impossible.

The depression led to more militant politics at state level. Prior to 1874 the Republicans had controlled nearly all the Northern state governments. After 1873, however, farmers, especially in the West, flooded into the co-operative movement known as the National Grange of the Patrons of Husbandry, founded in 1867 by Oliver Kelley. (Its members were popularly called Grangers.) The Granger movement's main aim initially had been to provide social and cultural benefits for isolated rural communities and to establish co-operatives so that farmers could market their own crops and buy farm machinery without paying huge interest rates on bank loans. But as farm prices collapsed and many farmers in states like Iowa and Illinois found themselves in debt, the movement - some 800,000 strong by 1874 - became more political. Grange members, complaining that railroad companies set charges that discriminated against small customers, demanded regulation of the railroads: some also favoured currency inflation to raise agricultural prices and enable indebted farmers to meet their mortgage payments. The Grangers also agitated on behalf of agricultural research, better schools and more equitable tax rates. In a number of Western states,

Granger coalitions united Democrats with disgruntled Republican farmers and it seemed that the mould of two party politics might be broken. In 1874 Granger political leaders won control of a number of Western state legislatures. These legislatures then tried to eliminate discriminatory railroad rates. In Illinois, for example, the state legislature set up a railroad commission to oversee railroad charges. The leading railroad companies protested, insisting that they were being deprived of property without due process of law. In the case Munn v Illinois (1877), the Supreme Court supported Illinois's stand. State legislatures could fix maximum charges: if the charges seemed unreasonable to the parties concerned, they should direct their complaints to the legislature or to the people, not to the courts.

Grant was not particularly concerned by the Granger movement (which began to decline as a major political force after 1876). He was more troubled by another major scandal - the whisky scandal - which hit his administration in 1875. Distillers and distributors made an almost routine practice of bribing Treasury tax agents to ignore the mismeasurement of bottled whisky or to supply tax stamps in excess of the amount paid for them. Massive amounts of money were involved and some 350 men in the government and the distilling industry were arrested. The whisky scandal tarnished Grant's administration because several people who were very close to the President were implicated, including his secretary Orville Babcock, Grant's own brother, his brother-in-law, and his eldest son. Grant knew that Babcock was guilty yet was prepared to perjure himself before the Chief Justice of the US to keep him out of jail. The whisky frauds deflected Grant's attention in his last two years in office from matters of far greater importance. He did nothing, for example, to prevent the counter-revolution in the South as white supremacists regained control in a number of states. (Eric Foner has particularly criticised him for failing to send federal troops into Mississippi in 1875 to support the state's Republican government.)

9 The 1876 Election

Grant was eager to run again in 1876 but, given the economic situation and the spate of recent scandals, Republican leaders saw him as a liability and were opposed to his standing. Instead, the Republican convention, meeting in Cincinnati, nominated Rutherford B. Hayes. With a distinguished Civil War record (wounded four times and promoted to Major General), and useful political experience (three times Governor of Ohio), Hayes seemed a strong candidate. An advocate of hard money and a supporter of civil service reform, he offended neither the radical nor the conservative wing of the Republican Party. The Democrat convention in St. Louis nominated Samuel Tilden, a millionaire corporation lawyer and reform Governor of New York. Tilden was renowned as the man who had directed the campaign to overthrow first the notorious Tweed Ring and then another ring in Albany which had cheated New York state of millions of dollars.

The campaign generated no burning issues. Both candidates favoured civil service reform and the trend toward conservative rule in the South. The Republicans essentially waved the bloody shirt. The Democrats, by contrast, attacked the Republican dirty linen and especially the failure and corruption of the Republican governments in the South. Hayes eventually triumphed in what remains the most corrupt American election since the Civil War (see pages 54-5). Months after balloting, it was not clear who had won. Eventually the disputed electoral votes of South Carolina, Louisiana and Florida were given to Hayes who became President by one electoral college vote (187-186). Hereafter Hayes's Democrat opponents invariably referred to him as 'His Fraudulence'.

Ironically, given his nickname and the manner in which he was elected, Hayes embodied morality. Honest, respectable, competent and dignified, the new President lived in modest style. His wife Lucy, a college-educated woman of great moral earnestness, actively supported the Women's Christian Temperance Union and soon became nicknamed 'Lemonade Lucy' because of her refusal to serve strong drink on social occasions at the White House. Hayes went some way to restoring respect for the office of President after the scandals of Grant's administration. Politically temperate and cautious, Hayes saw himself more as a caretaker than a leader. He felt that Congress should assume the main responsibility for determining national problems and had no intention of trying to be a President in the heroic mould.

Hayes did have some success in terms of placating the - white - South. But this success was the result of abandoning any pretence of trying to safeguard the position of Southern blacks. After 1877 white Democrats ruled in every Southern state.

Long a critic of the spoils system, Hayes supported civil service reform, promising in his inaugural address 'thorough, radical and complete' reform. While he failed to get legislation on the subject, many of his appointments were men of intelligence and integrity and he refused to allow powerful, patronage-minded Republican leaders to dictate his selections. But he did not fully implement the merit principle and the number of appointments he made as rewards for political services, seriously compromised him with reformers.

On the economic issues of the day Hayes took a conservative line. His solution to labour troubles, demonstrated in the Great Railroad Strike of 1877 (see page 83), was to send in the troops and break the strike. He took a hard money position and was opposed to increasing the money in circulation by issuing more greenbacks or supporting the new panacea - unlimited coinage of silver at a ratio of 16 to one to gold.

10 Conclusion

It is easy to be critical of American politics and politicians in the Gilded Age. There was immorality at every level of politics. Money had massive influence. Many politicians, including President Grant, were in politics to make a living and if possible to get rich. Party leaders and party machines were often not concerned with matters of principle. For them the whole point of politics was winning or holding office and distributing patronage. But the majority of Northern politicians were not rogues. Many had served with real distinction in the Civil War. Most were vigorous, intelligent, capable and public-spirited men - and devout patriots who believed in a glorious future for the USA. In many respects they well represented their constituents. Most Americans did not expect federal - or state - governments to intervene too actively in economic and social matters. Most cherished notions of laissez-faire, individualism, free-enterprise and limited government. The majority of Americans seem to have enjoyed politics - which was a kind of national game. Most who could vote did vote. The major issues of the time were thoroughly discussed - and many of those issues were important ones which still divide politicians today.

In some respects it is difficult to claim that the Civil War had a major effect on American politics. Even the corruption of the Gilded Age was nothing new: it had existed long before the war - and continued well into the twentieth century. The war did little to change the operation of the Constitution. During the war Lincoln had greatly expanded the power of the presidency, which, given he was Commander-in-Chief, he had been able to do. But this expansion of presidential power was not permanent. After 1865 the balance of power swung away from the executive branch. This was partly the result of the Congressional assault on Johnson. It was also the result of Grant's abdication of authority. Grant's successors - Hayes, Garfield, Arthur, Cleveland, Harrison and Cleveland again - all took a similar line, sharing the prevailing belief that the President should confine himself to executing the laws, leaving the making of them to Congress. Nor did the war have much effect on the federal-state balance. The war had been waged to uphold federal sovereignty. However, after 1865 individual states continued to have more power over Americans' daily lives than the federal government, which quickly jettisoned many of the functions it had assumed during the war. Along with conscription and all the other apparatus for raising and sustaining a huge army, the federal government discarded most of the wartime sources of revenue, slashed its own expenditures and scaled down the attempt to manage the nation's financial system. It accepted strict limitations of its power. When people did want help from the government, they tended to turn first to local or state authorities. Some of the fiercest political contests were fought far from Washington - for example, the farmers' demands for state legislation to regulate what they thought were exorbitant railroad rates. Prohibition remained an important issue that was largely fought out at state level.

However, some things had changed. Both the war and the programme of Congressional reconstruction asserted the supremacy of the federal government over the individual states. Nor did the federal government shed all its wartime weight. Federal expenditure and revenue after 1865 remained well above the pre-war levels. The national banking system survived and even the greenback continued a somewhat precarious existence. Wartime legislation on the tariff, public lands and railroads was consolidated, not abandoned after 1865.

After 1865 a new generation of Northern politicians came to the fore. Many of these men were war heroes. Some of them might have become leading politicians with or without the war. But others, like Grant, would surely not have made it to the top but for the war. The war also determined the way most Northerners continued to vote. One topic obsessed Northern politicians in the decades after 1865. That was the 'bloody shirt' which the historian Paul Buck has called 'possibly the greatest weapon any American party ever possessed'. The term referred to the tactic of reminding the Northern electorate that the men who had taken the South out of the Union and precipitated the Civil War had been Democrats, and that their descendants were still Democrats. Should their party regain power, former rebels would run the government and undo all the work accomplished at such sacrifice during the war. 'Every man that endeavoured to tear down the old flag,' a Republican orator proclaimed in 1876, 'was a Democrat. Every man that tried to destroy this nation was a Democrat... The man that assassinated Abraham Lincoln was a Democrat... Soldiers, every scar you have on your heroic bodies was given you by a Democrat.' Virtually every Republican candidate, decent and not so decent, waved the bloody shirt after 1865, ensuring that the Republican Party remained the North's 'natural' ruling party - an object of intense devotion for many Northerners. The Democrats had been the dominant political party for most of the period from 1800 to 1860. In the 70 years after 1860 only two Democrat Presidents - Cleveland and Wilson - occupied the White House. The Republican Party lived for decades on its reputation as the party which saved the Union and freed the slaves - the party of Abraham Lincoln. Perhaps the most important political result of the Civil War was that the North dominated American politics after 1865 and the Republican Party dominated the North.

Making notes on 'Northern Political Developments, 1865-77'

It is worth re-reading your notes on chapters 2 and 3 before commencing making notes on this chapter. Your notes on all three chapters should give you an understanding of the main political developments under Presidents Johnson and Grant. Chapters 2 and 3 examined Johnson and Grant's reconstruction policies in the South and the effect those policies had on the overall political scene. This chapter looks at the main political developments in the North. Your notes on this chapter should help you answer the following questions:

1 What impact did the Civil War have on Northern - and thus national - political development?
2 Was this so-called Gilded Age a period of terrible corruption and cynicism?

Your notes should also give you an understanding of the following - subsidiary - questions:

3 What did the Republican Party stand for?
4 Why did Grant win the 1868 presidential election?
5 Why was Grant re-elected in 1872?
6 What (reconstruction apart) were the main political issues of the period?

Source-based questions on '*Northern Political Developments, 1865-77*'

1 Hard Money
Read the extract from Grant's inaugural speech on pages 102-3. Answer the following questions:
a) According to the extract, what were Grant's main reasons for supporting hard money? (3 marks)
b) How might a soft money advocate have responded to Grant's speech? (4 marks)
c) What other policies does Grant indicate, in this extract, that he might support? (3 marks)

2 Political Issues in the Gilded Age
Read Lord Bryce's account on page 96 and part of the Liberal Republican platform on page 107. Examine the 1872 election posters on page 108. Answer the following questions:
a) What might be the strengths and weaknesses of Lord Bryce's source in helping historians understand the political situation in the Gilded Age? (5 marks)
b) Comment on the type of appeal that the Republican poster was making to the electorate in 1872. (4 marks)
c) Comment on the type of appeal that the Liberal Republican poster was making to the electorate in 1872. (4 marks)
d) Why was Civil Service reform seen as an important issue in 1872? (4 marks)
e) What do the four sources together suggest about the state of American politics in the 1870s? (8 marks)

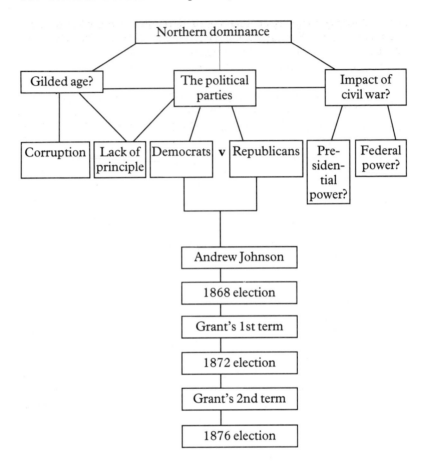

Summary - Northern Political Developments, 1865-77

CHAPTER 6

The Winning of the West

1 Introduction

By 1860 the United States' Western frontier lay some way beyond the Mississippi - an irregular line of settlement from St Paul, Minnesota in the North to Fort Worth, Texas in the South. But settlers had also leapfrogged across the continent to establish a bridgehead on the Pacific coast in California and Oregon. Between these two frontiers lay 1,500 miles of wilderness, comprising nearly half the North American continent - 1.25 billion acres of land. This area, called the 'Great American Desert' in mid-nineteenth century American atlases, was actually made up of three distinct regions: the Great Plains stretching 1,300 miles from Canada to Texas; the Rocky Mountains and the Sierra Nevadas; and between these two areas the Great Basin, a region of high grassy plateaux and deserts. These great expanses were the home of numerous Indian tribes and immense herds of buffalo. Apart from a Mormon settlement in Utah, the only whites in the region were traders, prospectors and trappers - people who were often as far removed from the ways of white civilisation as the Indians and just as nomadic. In the early nineteenth century many Americans believed that the area between the Mississippi and the Rockies was a waste - unsuitable for agriculture and uninhabitable by white settlers. The Great Plains, flat and sparsely vegetated, seemed particularly forbidding. There were few trees to provide shelter, fuel, fences or shade. The climate of the Plains was extreme - hot in summer and bitterly cold in winter. An added problem was the low and unpredictable rainfall. The fact that Plains Indians were prepared to wage savage resistance in defence of their homelands was an added problem. Nevertheless, in the two decades before the Civil War, white farmers had begun to settle on the fertile prairies of Iowa, Minnesota, Kansas and Nebraska, and prospectors had begun to mine gold in both the Rockies and the Sierras.

The effect of the Civil War on Western development is a subject of some debate. It is possible to claim that the War slowed down the western advance of farmers. Given the need for soldiers in the east, it might appear that the United States lacked the military means to defend western settlers from Indian attack. However, the Civil War seems to have had little effect on the easterly advance of the mining frontier. (Most miners moved east - into the so-called 'West' - from California and Oregon.) The war itself hardly touched the lives of most Indians, Mexicans, Asians, trappers, miners and Mormons scattered across the plains and mountains. It is possible that political developments during the War, not least the passing of the Homestead Act and Congressional support for a transcontinental railroad (see below), encouraged the Western development that occurred in the years after 1865. But it is difficult to believe that this development would not have otherwise occurred. In overall terms, therefore, the Civil War seems to have had remarkably little impact on the remorseless advance of white settlers westwards (and eastwards!).

On one level, the settlement of the - wild - West in the two decades after 1865 constitutes a colourful drama of determined pioneers, usually of modest means - war veterans, immigrants from Germany, Scandinavia and Britain, and American farming families from further east - overcoming all obstacles to secure their visions of freedom and opportunity. This romantic vision of Western history has long had a grip on the American, indeed on world, imagination. But on another level the settlement - or colonisation - of the West was a tragedy of short-sighted greed and irresponsible behaviour, resulting in reckless exploitation that nearly exterminated a people, scarred the region's landscape and almost wiped out several of its species of wild animals. This chapter will examine the reality of the Wild West and attempt to explain why the Western advance occurred at such a phenomenal rate in the 1860s and 1870s.

2 The Impact of Government Action

In many ways the American government had limited control over the process of Western expansion. Indeed, it is almost possible to claim that this expansion went ahead in spite of the government. However, despite appearances, the federal government by no means washed its hands of Western developments. The fact that the government had clear rules defining the process by which Western areas were incorporated into the United States was of pivotal importance. These rules had been established in the late eighteenth century. Newly settled Western areas first became territories, under the control of the federal government. When the territories had enough settlers, a territorial convention could draw up a constitution and apply to become a fully-fledged state. Most American politicians favoured Western expansion. Most thought it was America's manifest destiny to control the whole North American continent. While many Congressmen had some sympathy with the Native Americans, the federal government was prepared to use its armed forces to support white settlers against the Indians. Throughout the period, the American government tried to maintain control of overall Indian policy.

The federal government had less impact on Western economic development. Nevertheless, two pieces of legislation passed by the Republican-controlled Congress during the Civil War were to have a major effect on Western development after 1865. One was the 1862 Pacific Railroad Act: the other was the 1862 Homestead Act.

The settlement of Oregon and California in the 1840s had resulted in considerable support for a transcontinental railroad in the years before the Civil War. The colossal expense involved in building such a railroad meant that federal aid was essential. Prior to 1861, sectional jealousies prevented Congress taking action: Southern Congressmen had demanded a Southern route; Northerners had pressed for a Northern or central route. The secession of the Confederate states enabled Northerners to agree on a central route. The July 1862 Pacific Railroad Act chartered the Union Pacific Company to build westward across the continent from Omaha and authorised the Central Pacific Company to build eastward from Sacramento. Both companies were given (unprecedentedly) large land grants - a 400 foot right of way and 5 square miles of public land on each side of the track for each mile of track laid. The land was allotted in alternate sections, forming a pattern like a chess board: the squares of one colour represented railroad property: the squares of the other colour represented government property. The companies were also granted huge government loans varying in amount with the difficulty of the terrain. In 1864, with the project languishing apparently for want of capital, Congress doubled the land grant. Federal railroad policy was to have a major impact on Western development (see below).

The Civil War also enabled the Republicans to pass the 1862 Homestead Act. By this Act, a farmer could lay claim to 160 acres of Western land simply by living on it for five years. The prospect of free Western land seemed a good carrot to encourage farmers to press out onto the Great Plains.

Many Americans, particularly Westerners, like to believe that the West was won by rugged individuals successfully overcoming natural, human and economic obstacles, and that this success had little to do with government initiatives. There is some truth in this view. After 1865 most American politicians favoured laissez-faire government: they did not believe that governments should interfere overtly in economic and social matters; they supported individual enterprise. Nevertheless, federal government policy, especially with regard to Indians, land and railroads, had a major effect on Western expansion.

3 The Impact of the Railroads

Although the 1862 and 1864 Pacific Railroad Acts provided generous amounts of land and money, the building of the first transcontinental line did not really begin in earnest until after 1865. The government land grants and financial support ensured that money flowed in from both American and European investors. Nevertheless, the builders of the line faced formidable problems. Everything required had to be transported over long distances, together with food and supplies for the thousands of labourers employed in the construction work. The Union Pacific construction gangs were chiefly Irish immigrants and discharged Union soldiers: the Central Pacific relied heavily on imported Chinese labour. The Central Pacific faced the challenge of building a track across - or through - the Sierra Nevada mountains. The Union Pacific had an easier job building across the Great Plains but workmen had to be constantly on the lookout for marauding Indians. In May 1869 the two lines finally met at Promontory Point in Utah. The Union Pacific company had built 1,086 miles of track: the Central Pacific had built 689 miles.

The economic side of the transcontinental line was somewhat sordid. Unscrupulous shareholders of both railroad companies devised an ingenious scheme to enrich themselves. Instead of inviting competitive tenders, they created dummy construction companies to do the actual building; the Credit Mobilier for the Union Pacific and the Contract and Finance Company for the Central Pacific. This enabled them to charge exorbitant rates. In consequence the building companies made huge profits while the railroad companies were heavily burdened with debt. Moreover, the terms under which government aid was granted turned the transcontinental project into a race between the two railroads - simply to get federal money. This put a premium on speed of construction rather than quality. The result was that the lines of both companies soon had to be extensively resited and reconstructed.

Nevertheless, the completion of the first transcontinental railroad was

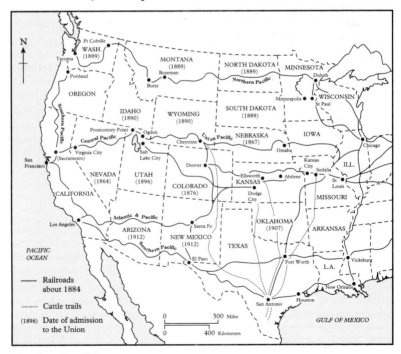

The American West

a remarkable feat of planning and engineering. It was not to be the last such feat. By the 1890s there were four other transcontinental lines. The building of these great east-west lines accounted for only a fraction of Western rail construction. Other lines were built north-south and all the railroad companies built a web of branch lines. Western rail mileage which had amounted to only 3,000 miles in 1865 had increased to 87,000 miles by 1900.

Although there were no more federal loans to railroads after 1873, all the transcontinental lines received lavish federal land grants. In all, the federal government gave the railroads 131 million acres - an area larger than Germany. The contribution of the federal government was matched by that of the individual state governments which advanced over $200 million and made land grants totaling 48 million acres.

A railroad advertisement for land, 1875

However, government aid, whether federal or state, should not be exaggerated. Most of the capital for railroad building came from the private sector - from European investors and New York banking houses. No railroad company waxed fat from the sale of its land grants: it took many years to sell all the land. Nevertheless, the government land grants were vitally important - not so much for the cash they realised (much of the land was not sold until the line itself was completed) as for the security for raising credit they provided, thus enabling construction work to start. The federal government benefited from its railroad-supporting policies. The railroads played a major role in opening up the West, ensuring that a flood of people moved in and an abundance of raw materials moved out of the West. The federal government also benefited financially from its land grant policy. The alternate sections of land it retained along the railroad track fetched twice the price of land elsewhere. Moreover, government traffic along the lines enjoyed a 50 per cent discount (and troops were to be carried free). Government railroad policy, therefore, proved to be shrewd and beneficial, given that prevailing attitudes prevented it from undertaking the work itself.

4 The Land Bonanza

In the years after 1865 farmers began to press out onto the Great Plains. Some took advantage of the 1862 Homestead Act. However, it was not easy to set up home on the free land. A great deal of capital (probably in the region of $1,000) was needed to move West, purchase the tools, seed, stock and machinery needed, and to survive for a year before the first crops could be harvested. Free Western lands, therefore, were not a 'safety valve' for poor industrial workers, most of whom did not have the money, the skills or the inclination to become farmers. Most Western homesteaders were already farmers, usually from districts not far removed from the frontier regions. Yet even for these experienced farmers, there were serious problems with the Homestead Act. The framers of the measure failed to realise that 160 acres was too small a unit on which to make a living on the Plains. Much of the land was only suited for cattle grazing - and cattlemen needed far more than 160 acres.

There were other problems with the Homestead Act, not least the fact that it quickly invited fraud. Many of the men who claimed free land had no intention of farming the land themselves: they were dummy registrants acting for speculators, cattlemen, mining or lumber companies who were simply trying to acquire as much land as they could. The result was that much of the 274 million acres claimed under the Act passed quickly to large concerns. Subsequent land laws (e.g. the 1873 Timber Culture Act, which permitted individuals to claim an additional 160 acres if they agreed to plant a quarter of it with trees within ten years, and the 1877 Desert Land Act, which allowed a settler to buy 640 acres at $1.25 an acre provided the holding was irrigated within two years) did not really help the small homesteader. Most measures of this kind were adopted largely in response to pressure from ranchers and lumber interests intent on plundering the public domain.

The Homestead Act and subsequent federal measures contributed far less to the settlement of the West than the colonising activities of states and railroads. Western states and territories made strenuous attempts to promote settlement, stationing agents in the East and in Europe to advertise opportunities for settlers. But even these quite considerable efforts were overshadowed by those of the land-grant railroad companies. Having millions of acres for sale and seeing in settlement a means of generating rail traffic, railroads spent lavishly in attempts to attract settlers from both Eastern states and Europe. Their promotional literature depicted the West as a land of milk and honey. In addition, they held out a variety of inducements: long-term loans, reduced steamship rates and free 'land-exploring tickets'. Railroad advertising proved remarkably effective. Large numbers of immigrants were lured to the Great Plains from Britain, Germany and Scandinavia. Many of these groups clustered together to form compact homogeneous settlements so that by 1890 hundreds of tiny German, Swedish and British 'colonies' were dotted across the West. But the majority of settlers were from American states further east.

Despite the glowing descriptions of the colonisation literature, newcomers soon discovered that the treeless and arid Plains presented great difficulties. For the first arrivals, life was often a grim struggle with danger and adversity, and involved long hours of back-breaking work in isolated surroundings. Given the lack of wood, farmers were forced to build their houses out of sods of earth and had to rely on dried dung for fuel. The nearest neighbours were often miles away. Pioneer families fought a constant battle with the elements - tornadoes, hailstorms, droughts, prairie fires, blizzards and pests. Swarms of locusts would sometimes cover the ground six inches deep, consuming everything in their path. If land was relatively cheap, horses, livestock, wagons, wells, fencing, seeds and fertiliser were not. Freight charges and interests rates on loans seemed cripplingly high. The grueling conditions wore down many farmers and their families. The high transiency rate on the frontier reflected the frequent failure to adapt to the new environment.

Nevertheless, some of those farmers who weathered the lean, early years eventually came to identify closely with the land. Some remote farm settlements blossomed into thriving communities, complete with churches, libraries, hotels and social clubs. Farmers often pooled their energies, helping each other as best they could. Co-operation was a practical necessity - a form of insurance in a rugged environment where almost everyone was vulnerable to instant misfortune or economic disaster. Some Western farmers did prosper as many of the pressing problems were overcome. The problem of fencing, for example, was solved in 1873 when an Illinois farmer, Joseph Gliddon, put barbed wire on the market. For the first time it became possible to fence land cheaply. Deeply-drilled wells and steel windmills provided a steady if sometimes scant water supply, while 'dry farming' - a method of tillage involving deep ploughing and frequent harrowing - served to hold water in the soil. As the railroads arrived bearing lumber from wooded regions, farmers built more substantial houses. New ploughs and improvements in farm machinery lightened the burden of labour and ensured that western agriculture could be made to pay. Large farms, in particular, prospered, often becoming larger as they did so. In Minnesota and the Dakotas, the gigantic 'bonanza farms' with machinery for mass production became one of the marvels of the age. These farms sometimes over 10,000 acres in size and employing dozens of men, were usually controlled by wealthy corporations which employed able managers to run the farms at a profit. The best known farm manager was Oliver Dalrymple, hired in 1875 by the North Pacific Railroad to establish a model large-scale farm. By 1880 Dalrymple had 25,000 acres under crop and a paid-up team of some 80-100 men at harvest time.

The Eastern Plains from Minnesota and North Dakota down to Texas emerged as the wheat belt, the new breadbasket for both the USA and Europe, in the decades after the Civil War. The production of wheat in the USA nearly tripled in the years between 1865 and 1877 and wheat provided the great export crop which evened the USA's balance of payments and spurred economic growth. The population of the Middle Border and Northern Plains steadily increased. Between 1860 and 1900 the number of people in Kansas, Nebraska, the Dakotas, Iowa and Minnesota rose from less than one million to more than seven million. Like other exploiters of the nation's Western resources, the farmers took what they could from the soil, often with little heed for preserving its fertility and preventing erosion.

Given the fact that much of the cereal crop was exported, Western farmers' success depended increasingly on international market forces. Farmers were also dependent on other Americans. Bankers and loan companies provided the capital to expand farm operations and purchase machinery in good years. Middlemen stored - and sometimes sold - the farmers' produce. Railroads carried the goods to market. Farmers were unable to determine the price of things they bought and sold and most suffered in the 1870s as cereal prices tumbled as a result of a glut on the American and world markets. Corn, which had sold for 78c a bushel in 1867, had fallen to 31c a bushel by 1873. Farmers who had borrowed heavily to finance their homestead and to purchase new machinery went bankrupt. Many small farmers believed that the 'system' of corrupt middlemen and avaricious bankers and railroad companies conspired against them.

The situation was not so simple. The years after 1873 saw the entire American economy caught in a grinding depression in which railroad operators and middlemen also had to struggle to survive. Although farm prices were falling, so too were prices of manufactured goods and railroad rates - often faster than farm prices. Interest rates too were falling, so there was plenty of credit available.

5 The Cattle Bonanza

By no means all Western farmers were concerned with cereal production. Cattle provided a livelihood for many - and a spectacularly good livelihood for a few - in the two decades after the Civil War. In 1865 some entrepreneurs realised there was no need to breed or stock their own cattle. On the rich grasslands of Texas an estimated 5 million longhorn cattle roamed free and unowned. These cattle could be had just for the effort of rounding them up. They were worth $30 to $40 dollars a head if they could be sold to Northern meat markets - ten times the price which beef fetched in Texas. For Texas cattle to reach the Northern markets, they first had to reach a convenient point on a railroad (a railhead) from which they could be sent (usually first) to St Louis and then to Chicago. In 1866 some enterprising Texans headed a large herd northwards on the first post-war so-called 'long drive' - a 1,000 mile trek across the open range to a railhead in Missouri. Joseph McCoy, one of three brothers already in the livestock business in Illinois, was one of many who realised the Texas potential. Helped by the liberalisation of the Kansas cattle quarantine laws in 1867 (the result of a well-organised cattlemen's lobby), McCoy developed a more suitable railhead at Abilene in Kansas. In 1867 35,000 head of cattle trudged along the Chisholm Trail to Abilene. In 1868 this number doubled and by 1871 700,000 cattle reached Abilene. Overnight Abilene grew from a place with just a few log huts into the first flourishing Kansas cowtown.

As the railroads and farming frontiers extended further westwards into the Great Plains, new trails came into being, new railheads eclipsed Abilene, and new cowtowns developed - Ellsworth, Wichita and Dodge City. Between 1866 and 1888 some 6 to 10 million cattle were driven to the cattle towns where they were shipped to the packing centres of the Middle West. Other herds, however, were driven on a second long drive to be fattened on the Northern Plains or to stock the ranches of Colorado, Wyoming, Montana and the Dakotas.

During the 20 years after the Civil War some 40,000 cowboys roamed the Great Plains. Most were in their teens or early twenties. They came from diverse backgrounds. Many were restless ex-Confederate soldiers seeking adventure. Perhaps a third were Mexican, African or Native Americans. Most worked as cowboys for a year or two and then drifted into other livelihoods. Many were strong, silent men - self-reliant, individualistic and contemptuous of authority. Some were skilled marksmen and most could certainly protect themselves. Virtually all were expert horsemen, an essential skill given that cowboys virtually lived on horseback for the two months that most cattle drives took. But cowboy life was rarely as glamorous as the dime novel of the time or cinema and television since has depicted it. For a wage of only $25 to $30 a month, the average cowboy worked an 18 hour day trying to control and coax forward a sprawling mass of cattle, coping with a continuous cloud of dust, and facing a variety of other potential hazards - floods, poisonous snakes and scorpions, blizzards, stampedes, rustlers, and occasionally Indians. At journey's end, cowboys not surprisingly often whooped it up in the saloons and bordellos of the cattle towns. However, the cattle towns were generally less riotous than Western mining settlements. Saloons were no more numerous than pubs in similar-sized towns in late nineteenth-century Britain. (Abilene had only eleven saloons in 1871, its busiest cattle season.) The number of murders in the cattle towns has also been greatly exaggerated. The 25 or so violent deaths that helped fill 'Boot Hill' cemetery during Dodge City's first year as a community pre-dated the era of the long drive. During its 10 years as a cattle town (from 1875 to 1884) Dodge City witnessed a total of only 15 murders - low by frontier standards. Indeed, law and order usually accompanied the rise of the cattle trade. Courts were established, laws passed, and professional gunmen sometimes employed to serve as police-officers.

Few cowboys grew rich but some men did make their fortunes from the cattle drives. The drives, however, were relatively short-lived. The fact that cattle could be fattened for market on the Great Plains led to the replacement of the range by the ranch. By 1880 ranching had spread northwards from Texas as far as Canada. The long cattle drive received a number of severe blows. The appearance of splenic fever among cattle in the stockyards of Kansas City, St. Louis and Chicago, prompted the passage of more stringent state quarantine laws. The production of barbed wire for fencing encouraged ranching and was, in many ways, the death knell of the open range. The spread of railroad lines across the West also made ranching more cost effective.

Huge tracts of grazing land were quickly appropriated by cattle ranchers who often resorted to fraud and perjury in order to obtain sufficient amounts of land for pasture. Water rights were usually more important than land rights: whoever controlled the water, effectively controlled the land. Disputes over land and water rights and rustling of livestock were endemic and often led to violence between rival ranchers. Vigilante systems quickly sprang up, providing mutual protection and a measure of order. Leading ranchers also banded together to form livestock associations which developed a code of rules defining land and water rights and the recording of brands. In most cases the associations, which assumed quasi-governmental powers in the territories, seem to have operated reasonably effectively and fairly. But they were by no means universally popular. Some behaved arbitrarily and sometimes unjustly, often favouring big ranchers at the expense of small. The livestock industry, like many other American industries in the late nineteenth century, was increasingly dominated by 'big business'.

Western cattle made up a growing but still relatively small percentage of overall cattle numbers in the USA: 3 per cent in 1870 and only 10 per cent in 1880. The greatest boom in the range-cattle trade came in the early 1880s when Eastern and European investors poured money into the 'Beef Bonanza'. (By 1883, for example, British companies owned or controlled nearly 20 million acres of Western grazing land.) It seemed that large profits could be made with relatively small investment. Inevitably, the ranges became grossly over-crowded and beef prices tumbled. Two exceptionally severe winters in 1885-6 and 1886-7, straddling a terrible summer drought, resulted in the death of millions of Western cattle (possibly 90 per cent of the total). Thousands of cattlemen were ruined and the disaster was a lethal blow to the open-range livestock business. Most of the cattlemen who survived retreated into the security of a fenced-in ranch, equipped with shelter against the elements. Cowboys, in effect, became farmhands and they only rode that part of the range which was owned by their employer.

6 The Sheep Bonanza

In some territories, particularly those in the foothills of the Rockies, there was a sheep rather than a cattle bonanza. In many Western territories sheep-boys were probably more typical than cowboys. Cattlemen and sheep ranchers sometimes (literally) fought for control of water holes and grazing rights. Sheep were reputed to pollute precious drinking water and to ruin pasture by close cropping. The prolonged warfare which reached its height in the 1880s resulted in the deaths of dozens of cattlemen and sheep-herders.

7 The Mining Bonanza

In the Western mountains, miners usually paved the way for other settlers. Whenever anyone made a 'strike', prospectors flocked to the site, drawn by rumours and dreams of riches. The excitement of the California gold rush of 1848-9 was re-enacted time and again in the following three decades. In 1858-9 the discovery of gold in Colorado resulted in the Pike Peak rush: by 1860 there were some 35,000 people in the region. At the same time the Comstock Lode - the greatest single deposit of precious metals ever found in the USA - was discovered in Nevada. (Within 20 years the Lode had yielded more than $300 million in gold and silver.) The encroachments of miners on the West continued through the Civil War, especially in Montana and Arizona. In the early 1870s gold was found in the Black Hills of Dakota, sparking a great rush onto territory owned by Native Americans: both the Indians and the US army found it impossible to exclude prospectors. In 1877 discovery of the Lucky Cuss silver mine in Arizona sparked yet another rush. Frustration, hardship and back-breaking labour were the lot of most miners: only a tiny fraction succeeded in striking it rich. Nevertheless, despite repeated disappointments, thousands of prospectors spent their lives in an obsessive but elusive search for gold.

The sudden disorderly rush of prospectors to a new find led to mining towns springing up overnight. Most of the first inhabitants of towns like Virginia City, Nevada (described in Mark Twain's *Roughing It*), Deadwood, Dakota, and Tombstone, Arizona, were young, transient, adventurous and cosmopolitan males. Such towns, which quickly attracted saloon-keepers, prostitutes and assorted desperadoes, established notorious reputations for debauchery and violence. By 1873 Virginia City, which grew up as a result of the discovery of the Comstock Load, had 20,000 inhabitants. Men outnumbered women by three to one and the town had 131 saloons and numerous brothels. Deadwood, in its brief heyday, was one of the most lawless spots on earth. According to the historian Ray Allen Billington, in Deadwood 'the faro games were wilder, the hurdy-gurdy dance halls noisier, the street brawls more common, than in any other Western town'. Gunfights were commonplace. However, it does seem that most men adhered to a rough code of conduct. Most of those who were involved in shoot-outs chose to be involved. Women, children, elderly citizens and those unwilling to fight were rarely the targets of attack. Indeed, they were often safer in the mining towns than they would have been in cities in the East.

Although the mining towns were notorious for their turbulence, it was only in the first year or so that crime, disorder and vice flourished. As in the cattle towns, the law-abiding and responsible majority quickly took matters into their own hands. Informal codes of law were established and rough and ready justice meted out by groups of vigilantes. Although these groups have often had a bad press, they were perhaps the only effective weapon against organised crime and generally seem to have meted out justice at least as fairly as the official system. A few summary hangings usually drove the 'bad men' out of town. The forces of respectability ensured that those towns which survived soon had stable communities. Schools, churches and newspaper offices quickly came to outnumber the saloons and brothels. However, many of the towns that sprang up in the 1860s and 1870s disappeared almost as quickly as they had risen.

In the initial stages of mining development, individual prospectors could hope to make themselves rich simply by sifting off dirt and gravel from surface deposits of gold by panning. But once the rich surface metals had tailed off, efficient mining required shafts sunk into the ground and crushing mills built to extract the precious metal locked in quartz. Deep level quartz-mining required extensive outlays of capital: it also required considerable engineering skill. Western mining thus quickly became big business as most of the mining wealth fell into the hands of investment bankers and mining company owners. The mines around Deadwood, for example, were soon controlled by one large company, Homestake Mining. By 1880 the wild rush of individual prospectors had given way to organised enterprises. Most miners either moved on, settled down to work for the mining bosses or took up farming.

8 The Indian Wars

Almost from the moment the first white settlers arrived in America, Native Americans had been forced from their land and driven westwards. Convinced of their own cultural superiority, most whites saw nothing unjust in appropriating Indian hunting and agricultural land. Nevertheless, on the eve of the Civil War, Indians were still free to roam over half of the total area that is today the USA. But in the two decades after 1860, as farmers, miners and the railroads pressed in from east and west, the Native Americans were remorselessly driven into their last strongholds. In the 1860s there were three main Indian groups: the fierce Plains Indians; the weak and primitive tribesmen who inhabited the deserts between the Rockies and the Sierra Nevadas; and the peaceful farmers and herders of the Southwest. The last two groups were few in number and played little part in the coming conflict. It was the Plains Indians who offered the most implacable and sustained resistance to the advance of the white settlers.

In 1860 there are thought to have been some 250,000 Plains Indians, belonging to a great many distinct tribes. The Northern Plains, from the Dakotas and Montana south to Nebraska, were dominated by tribes which spoke the Sioux language as well as by Flatheads, Blackfeet, Northern Cheyennes, Arapahos and Crows. On the Central and Southern Plains were the so-called five Civilised Tribes, driven from the homelands in Georgia and the south-east in the 1830s, and forced to settle in the area known as Indian Territory (present day Oklahoma). Further west were the Pawnees, the Comanches, the Kiowas and the Southern Arapahos. Some of these tribes were traditional allies. Others were bitter enemies - the enmity arising from cultural differences, blood feuds or disputes over hunting grounds. Such divisions prevented the Indians from presenting a united front against the common foe. Moreover, Indians rarely met as a full tribe. Most lived in bands of about 300-500 people. These bands were largely autonomous and usually had little to do with each other. It was quite common for some bands to be at war while others bands of the same tribe were at peace.

Although divided, the Plains Indians were a dangerous foe. They lived mainly off the herds of buffalo which roamed the Western Plains. The buffalo provided most of the Indians' needs: especially food, clothing and shelter. The Indians' nomadic way of life made them

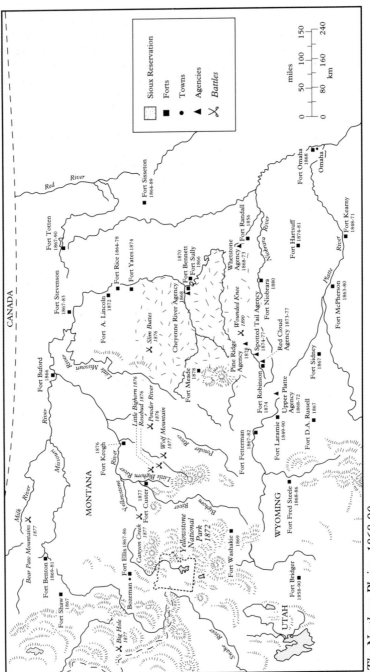

The Northern Plains, 1868–90

singularly elusive. Their hunting skills honed keen their military skills: in particular they were superb horsemen. War absorbed a great part of the energies of the Plains Indians. Indian youths were taught that war was the noblest of all activities - a test of manhood and honour. To die fighting in battle was the highest fulfilment since it ensured a happy afterlife. Both in battle and afterwards, Indian warriors were utterly ruthless. They scalped their dead foes and were likely to torture captives to death. (Torture was regarded as a means whereby a captive might acquire a badge of honour and show himself worthy of divine protection.) Not surprisingly white settlers feared hostile Indians. Man for man Indian warriors were probably better than US soldiers. But unit for unit, the Indians did not match the discipline and organisation of the American army, which was supported by a far more sophisticated and technological society.

Wars between Indians and US troops raged intermittently on the Plains from the 1860s to the 1880s. The Civil War might be thought to have given the Indians a chance. In 1861-2 regular troops were pulled out of the West for service in the East. Some Indians thought they had driven the white soldiers away. This was not so. Western volunteer militia units, mainly from California, replaced regular troops: by 1865 there were some 20,000 soldiers in the West, almost double the 1860 figure. The Western militia units - energetic, anti-Indian and led by some tough and aggressive generals - were possibly more of a threat to the Indians than the regular army. The fact that so many troops were committed to the West in the Civil War indicates the importance that President Lincoln's government attached to both Western gold and Western political support for the prosecution of the war. Lincoln left Indian affairs almost entirely to Congress and the Indian Bureau. While William Dole, the Commissioner of Indian Affairs, attempted to

'Flankers keeping Buffalo from Stampeding the Train and Column' from sketches by Holtes

promote humanitarian policies of reservation and Christianisation, Westerners dominated Congressional Indian committees. Most Western Congressmen favoured a military policy to destroy the Plains Indians.

During the Civil War the first serious Indian trouble developed in Minnesota in 1862 when federal authorities failed to give the Dakota Sioux their yearly supplies. Driven by hunger and angered by broken promises, Sioux tribesman wrought havoc on the frontier, killing or capturing some 1,000 whites: hundreds more fled to the safety of the nearest settlement or fort. Indian forces attacked Fort Ridgely and New Ulm but, at both places, the defenders turned back the assaults. White militia units soon went on the attack, defeating the Indians and inflicting a devastating revenge in the process. Some 2,000 Indians were captured and over 300 sentenced to death by a military commission. Lincoln pardoned the majority of the condemned men but eventually 38 were hanged in a mass execution in December 1862. The Dakota Sioux lost their reservations in Minnesota and were exiled to poor quality reservation land further West.

In 1864, forces led by Kit Carson defeated the Navajos in New Mexico and forced them onto reservation land. In Colorado, where the chiefs of the Cheyennes and Arapahos accepted a treaty banishing them westward, protesting braves began sporadic raids on the trails and mining camps. In 1864 the territorial governor persuaded most of the Indians to gather at Fort Lyon on Sand Creek, where they were promised protection. Despite this promise, a militia unit led by Colonel Chivington attacked the camp slaughtering hundreds of peaceful Indians - men, women and children. 'Kill and scalp all, big and little,' shouted Chivington, a former Methodist minister. 'Nits make lice.' Many Americans in the East were appalled at the massacre. But in the West Chivington and his men were acclaimed as heroes by most white citizens. (Chivington successfully exhibited his personal collection of a hundred Indian scalps in Denver.) In 1865 the Indian survivors surrendered unconditionally and gave up their Sand Creek reservation for lands further West.

In March 1865 Congress created a joint committee to investigate 'the condition of the Indian tribes and their treatment by the civil and military authorities of the United States'. Congress also authorised a treaty commission to approach the Sioux tribes of the upper Missouri. These two measures marked the first tentative steps towards a different kind of Indian policy - a policy of 'conquest by kindness' rather than by extermination. The federal government had no wish to stop Western expansion: it would have had difficulty doing so if it had wanted to. But many Easterners, while accepting as fact that whites would eventually occupy most of the West, felt sympathy for the Indians. Some of the nation's most powerful and respected citizens urged a peace policy and lobbied the government to that effect. Essentially, they advocated huge chunks of land being set aside as Indian reservations and efforts made to educate and civilise the Indians. Most Westerners, supported by the military authorities, felt no such sympathy: many continued to believe that the only good Indian was a dead one.

Throughout 1865 intermittent - but very bloody - clashes continued, keeping white areas in a state of alarm. Bands of Sioux, Cheyenne and Arapaho, often no more than ten to twenty strong, wiped out dozens of isolated white families and ambushed small army patrols on the Northern and Central Plains. Once the Civil War was over, thousands of regular troops took the offensive against the Indians: thousands more manned forts defending travel routes and settlements. While the frontier forts played a crucial role in establishing control of areas, large-scale military operations often had little success. Thousands of soldiers, operating in an inhospitable country, far from their base, required massive logistical support. Most troop columns, moving at the speed of their covered wagons, stood little chance of finding Indian bands to fight. Small, fast-moving army patrols, using mules for supplies and friendly Indians as scouts, were far more effective in locating and defeating hostile Indians.

From 1865 to 1867 the Indian leader Red Cloud led resistance to the army's attempt to build the Powder River Road (or Bozeman Trail) which would have cut across the best hunting grounds of the Western Sioux in Montana. Red Cloud's men harassed the soldiers so successfully that the road could not be built and most soldiers were bottled up in their forts. The Indians' greatest success came in December 1866 when 82 soldiers under Captain Fetterman were killed near Fort Phil Kearny.

The 'Fetterman Massacre' shocked the federal government into taking a fresh look at the Indian problem. Army chiefs, for the most part, urged vigorous military counter-measures: they wanted vengeance. Most scoffed at the notion of conquest by kindness. But Andrew Johnson's government and a majority in Congress supported a more compassionate solution. The Congressional Indian Committee, set up in 1865, finally reported in January 1867. It placed most of the blame for hostilities on white encroachments on Indian territory and favoured a reservation system and a deliberate policy to civilise the Indians thereafter. Congress was anxious for peace. The Indian wars were expensive: it cost $2 million a year to maintain a single regiment on the Plains and, according to one estimate, the government was spending a million dollars for each Indian actually killed in battle. In 1867 Congress set up a Peace Commission to tour the Plains and find a means of ending the fighting. The Commission, which included both civilian and military representatives, toured the territories, compiling its findings. Its 'Report on the Condition of the Indian Tribes', issued in January 1868, called for just and humane treatment of the Indians and an intensive programme to educate and civilise them. Although General Sherman and the other military representatives on the Commission did not like the evangelical and anti-military tone of the report, they signed it anyway, largely because it contained little to which they could plausibly object.

By 1868 the government had started to act on the Commission's findings. Efforts were made to persuade the tribes to settle on two large reservations, one, for the Sioux tribes, in the Black Hills of South Dakota; the other in Indian Territory (western Oklahoma) at the expense of the Five Civilised Tribes which would thus be punished for supporting the Confederacy in the Civil War. The government was also prepared to offer annuities, food and clothes to ease the Indians' transition to reservation life. Two great Indian conclaves were held, the first at Medicine Lodge Creek in October 1867 with the Southern Plains Indians, and the second at Fort Laramie in the spring of 1868 with the Northern Plains Indians. Most chiefs, realising that reservations offered the only alternative to extinction, yielded. But some did not and there was more hard fighting on the Southern Plains in 1868-9 as soldiers under the command of Civil War hero Philip Sheridan beat the Indians into submission. Sheridan had little sympathy for the Indians: 'The more we can kill this year,' he declared, 'the less will have to be killed next year. For the more I see of the Indian, the more convinced I am that all will have to be killed or maintained as paupers.' Sheridan ordered an autumn and winter campaign to force the Indians back onto the reservations. In November 1868 an army raiding party, commanded by Lieutenant Colonel George Armstrong Custer (another Civil War hero), attacked a Cheyenne village along the Washita River, killing over a hundred Indian warriors and forty women.

Meanwhile in 1869, spurred on by evangelical Christian reformers, Congress established a new civilian Board of Indian Commissioners, ending the long-standing division of authority between the Department of the Interior and the War Department. The Board's main purpose was to supervise conditions on the reservations, molding reservation life along the lines that the reformers - not the Indians - thought desirable. President Grant supported this reform policy. In his 1869 inaugural speech, he promised to 'favour any course ... which tends to ... [the] civilizing and ultimate citizenship' of the 'original occupants of this land'. Grant favoured the containment of tribes on reservations and hoped that educated Indians would become, in time, American citizens. In an effort to stamp out laxity and corruption among Indian agents, Grant tried to replace them, first with Quakers, then with nominees of other Protestant denominations. Such agents might help bring the Indians into the Christian fold. Grant seemed sympathetic to the Indians. One of his close friends and advisers, Colonel Ely Parker - a full-blooded Seneca Indian - was appointed to head the Commission of Indian Affairs. Grant's 'Peace Policy' delighted the Eastern reformers. The measures he supported were not new: they had long been advocated. What was new was their official adoption and a serious attempt to make them work.

Proclaiming high-sounding objectives in Washington was one thing; making them work out on the frontier was another. Unfortunately, the new system soon showed itself to be as inefficient as previous systems. The sheer bureaucratic complexity of translating Washington policy into field action confounded the efforts of able and well-meaning agents - and by no means all agents were well-meaning or efficient. Incompetent and corrupt officials slipped through the screen of missionary appointments in surprisingly large numbers. During Grant's presidency scandal after scandal rocked the agencies, bureau and department. An 'Indian Ring' in the Department of the Interior systematically stole the funds and supplies intended for the Indian reservations. In consequence, many Indians did not receive the welfare to which they felt entitled. (In 1871 Ely Parker, suspected of corruption, was forced to resign as Commissioner of Indian Affairs.) Army officers had to watch helplessly while civilian corruption and mismanagement prodded the Indians toward war. General Sherman, in overall command of Indian country, said: 'We could settle the Indian troubles in an hour, but Congress wants the patronage of the Indian bureau, and the bureau wants the appropriations without any of the trouble of the Indians themselves'. This was the army view. Military agents, it should be said, proved hardly more able or incorruptible than civilian officials. Given the lack of adequate funding, Indian agents found it difficult to keep Indians on the reservations where the wildlife was too sparse to support them. Even more serious was the fact that as the 1870s wore on army authorities found it just as hard to keep white settlers out of Indian territory.

Ironically, the eight years of Grant's Peace Policy were years of savage warfare. Within Indian tribes there was intense factionalism: while some chiefs continued to support peace and reservation, others favoured war. There were a number of bloody incidents. On the Southern Plains, a band of Kiowas, Comanches and Cheyennes raided the Adobe Walls trading post in Texas in 1874, sparking off the Red River War. Soldiers, in a fierce winter campaign, destroyed Indian supplies and slaughtered scores of Cheyenne fugitives near the Sappa River in Kansas. With the exile of the Indian 'ringleaders' to reservations in Florida, Indian independence on the Southern Plains came to an end.

The Northern Plains were a different matter. The Fort Laramie Treaty kept the Sioux relatively quiet for several years. In 1870 Red Cloud, pleased that the American government had agreed to stop work on the Bozeman Trail, led his Oglala Sioux people onto a reservation and never again took up arms against the whites. Peace with Red Cloud seemed a major victory for the Peace Policy. But some Sioux, Northern Cheyenne and Northern Arapaho had never been brought within the reservation system. These non-treaty Indians looked to the leadership of

Sitting Bull, a Hunkpapa Sioux chieftain, a religious as well as a political and war leader. The non-reservation Indians opposed continued white encroachment on their territory (in Dakota and Montana) and could count on the support of disenchanted warriors who had settled on the Great Sioux Reservation. In 1874 Colonel George Custer led an exploring expedition into the Black Hills of Dakota, accompanied by prospectors who found the gold they had been sent to find. Miners were soon filtering into the Sioux reservation hunting grounds and, despite promises to the contrary, the army did little to keep them out. In November 1875 negotiations to buy the Black Hills broke down because the Indian asking price was deemed too high.

Grant and his military advisers now decided to take no action to prevent miners streaming into the Black Hills. Grant's government also made it clear that any Indians outside the reservations by the end of January 1876 would be hunted down by the army. The Black Hills' situation set off an unusually large spring migration of reservation Indians to the camps of the non-treaty tribes, concentrated in the region of the Bighorn River in south Montana. By the summer of 1876 large numbers of Sioux were on the warpath and three columns of troops were sent to deal with the trouble. The commander of one of the columns, General Alfred Terry, sent a small detachment of the 7th Cavalry under

'Custers Last Stand'

The Battle of Little Bighorn. A contemporary Indian drawing by White Bear

George Custer ahead with orders to locate the Indian camp and block the Indian escape route through the Bighorn Mountains. In June Custer found the main Sioux and Cheyenne encampment on the Little Bighorn River. Some 8,000 Indians had gathered. Unaware of the exact size of the enemy camp, Custer, with some 250 men, rashly attacked. The 2,500 or so Indian warriors - the largest Indian army ever brought together in the USA - led by Crazy Horse and by Sitting Bull, fought back, killing Custer and his entire command. The battle is often referred to as 'Custer's Last Stand'. In reality, the battle of the Little Bighorn was the Sioux Indians' last stand. President Grant and the military authorities determined to avenge the Bighorn massacre and quash the Indian revolt. The army continued its remorseless pressure and shortages of food and ammunition soon forced most of the Sioux bands to surrender and return to the reservations.

After 1876 there were only a few sporadic outbreaks of violence on the Northern Plains. In 1877 the few Nez Perce tribesmen took to the warpath in the Rockies of Oregon and Idaho rather than surrender their lands. Their remarkable leader Chief Joseph conducted a retreat of 1,300 miles before being caught and taken prisoner by army forces just 30 miles short of the Canadian border. His eloquent speech of surrender was an epitaph of the warriors' last stand against the march of 'progress': 'I am tired of fighting. Our chiefs are killed... The old men are all dead. I want to have time to look for my children and see how many of them I can find. Hear me, my chiefs! I am tired. My heart is sick and sad. From where the sun now stands I will fight no more forever.' He and his people were uprooted from their traditional lands and settled on malarial-infested territory in far-off Oklahoma. In 1881, Sitting Bull, who had led his tribe to Canada after the battle of the Little Bighorn, finally surrendered. Both he and his tribe were forced to settle on a government reservation.

Fighting continued for a little longer in the extreme South. The Apaches in New Mexico and Arizona, had waged war against white settlers since Spanish colonial times and in the 1860s and 1870s attacked both Mexicans and Americans. In the early 1870s, General Crook seemed to be on the verge of ending the Apache wars. But many Apaches were not satisfied with the proffered reservation - a hot, barren malarial place - and two Apache leaders, Victorio and Geronimo, continued to fight. The wildness of the terrain - and the fact that it straddled the Mexican-American border - enabled the small bands of Apaches to hold out for several years. Victorio was finally defeated by Mexican forces. Geronimo continued to cause trouble for a few more years. His capture in 1886 brought an end to organised Indian resistance.

Indian resistance to white settlement was dramatic, heroic but ultimately futile. The few, disunited Indians never stood much chance of retaining their tribal lands against the overwhelming flood of white settlers. Those settlers were supported by a professional army and by far superior technology, which included the railroad, the electric telegraph and the Winchester repeating rifle. Although the Indians fought a skilful (and also savage) guerrilla-type war, leading army officers like Generals Sherman and Sheridan, toughened and brutalised by their Civil War experiences, were prepared to use equally savage methods. Winter campaigns proved particularly effective and most officers and men seem to have had little compunction in slaying Indian women and children. Army leaders also encouraged the wholesale killing of the buffalo herds, aware that this would make life difficult for the Indians. However, the destruction of the buffalo was not deliberately planned by the army: it was mainly the result of professional hunters killing the beast as food for railroad workers - or simply as sport. In the years 1872-4 some 3 million buffalo a year were probably killed. In 1865, there were two great buffalo herd on the Great Plains, comprising an estimated 13 million animals. By 1883 the southern herd had been exterminated and a scientific expedition could find only 200 survivors of the northern herd. The destruction of the buffalo meant the destruction of the Plains Indians' way of life.

By 1880 most Indians had been settled on reservations. Some had been moved several times. Chief Spotted Tail spoke for many when he said: 'Since the Great Father promised that we should never be removed, we have been moved five times... I think you had better put the Indians on wheels and you can run them about wherever you wish'. On paper, the reservations appeared large. Even after the cession of the Black Hills (which followed the 1876 war), the Great Sioux reservation which sprawled over South-west Dakota encompassed some 43,000 square miles. But farming and stock-raising was difficult on the Plains and reservation land was often poor and usually inadequate to meet Indian needs. In less than two decades, the Plains Indians' political, cultural, social and economic systems had been destroyed. The passing of the old ways undermined established beliefs and practices. The result was the moral and physical decline of a once proud people. Disease, alcoholism and poverty was the fate of most Indians.

Eastern politicians, churchmen and some of the leading humanitarians of the day continued to speak out against the mistreatment of Indians and did their best to ensure that Indians were treated justly. In 1877 newly-elected President Hayes accepted white responsibility and admitted: 'Many, if not most, of our Indian wars have had their origin in broken promises and acts of injustice on our part'. Under Hayes, renewed efforts were made to reform the Indian Bureau and prevent corruption. However, even those whites who were sympathetic to the Indians had little inclination to respect or preserve the 'savages'' way. Most liberal reformers, blind to any inherent value in the Indian life, believed that the best way forward was assimilation - so-called 'Americanisation' - and the eradication of Indian tribal culture.

Throughout the 1880s Congress appropriated more and more funds for Indian education. Boarding schools were established (the first at Carlisle, Pennsylvania in 1879) where Indian children might be isolated from parental influence and taught white American skills and attitudes. Indian religious practices were outlawed. Rations were withheld from those tribes which did not conform. The climax of the integrationist policy came with the Dawes General Allotment Act of 1887. This broke up reservation land into small units held by individuals or families. Each head of family could receive 160 acres of farmland; each single male adult 80 acres. Indians who accepted the 160 acre allotments and 'adopted the habits of civilised life' were to be granted United States citizenship after 25 years.

Reformers at the time hailed the Dawes Act as heralding a new era of harmony. But most twentieth-century historians have agreed that the effects of the measure were deplorable. As well as facilitating land grabbing by whites, it also shattered what was left of the Indian tribal structure. Most Indians found it hard to cope with American civilisation and were reduced to the status of almost complete dependency. Ironically both the humanitarian and the extermination advocates both played their part in shattering the Indian race and its ancient culture.

The last tragic epilogue came in 1890. All over the Northern Plains despairing Sioux Indians came to believe that if they took up a ceremonial dance at each new moon their lands and power would be restored. The Ghost Dance craze, feeding upon old legends of the coming of an Indian Messiah, spread rapidly and with such fervour that it soon alarmed white authorities. An effort to arrest Sitting Bull, one of the chiefs who was encouraging the Ghost Dance, led to his death. Bands of Sioux fled their reservations with the army in pursuit. In late December 1890, nervous 7th Cavalry fired into a group of Indians at Wounded Knee. Some 200 Indians - many of them women and children - and 25 soldiers died in the 'Battle of Wounded Knee'. Neither side had really wanted to fight. The whole affair - an accident born of mutual distrust, misunderstanding and fear - epitomised relations between Indians and white Americans in the late nineteenth century.

Not all American Indians suffered as severely as the Plains Indians. The pacific Pueblos in the South-west managed to retain their lands and their autonomy. The Five Civilised Tribes in the Oklahoma territory made a rapid recovery from the devastation and demoralisation resulting from the Civil War and the fact that they had supported the Confederacy. By 1880 the Five Tribes had attained a reasonable prosperity that set them apart from all other Western Indians. Interestingly, there was no Indian warfare in Alaska, America's last frontier. The 50-70,000 natives - Eskimo, Aleut and Indian - continued to live peacefully, so much so that in 1877 the few army units were withdrawn from the area. No treaty extinguished native title to land, no reservations were established, and no agency sought to impose a civilisation programme. This was largely because there was so much land and very little white incursion.

9 Conclusion

By 1890 the Western frontier had effectively gone. In 1890 the superintendent of the census noted that he could no longer locate a continuous frontier line beyond which population thinned out to fewer than two people per square mile. In the 1890s a young Wisconsin historian Frederick Jackson Turner claimed that the end of the frontier was the end of the first period of American history. In an 1893 lecture entitled 'The Significance of the Frontier in American History', Turner declared that the advance of American settlement westward explained American uniqueness. In Turner's view, the Anglo-Saxon frontiersmen's conquest of the Western frontier had shaped the national character in fundamental ways: it made Americans practical and inventive and led to 'dominant individualism', 'buoyancy and exuberance' and a belief in freedom. These were traits of the frontier - or traits resulting from the existence of the frontier. Turner's thesis - that the frontier was the source of America's democratic politics, open society, unfettered economy and rugged individualism - gripped the popular imagination in the early twentieth century. But Turner's 'frontier thesis' was, at best, a gross exaggeration. He over-emphasised the homogenising effect of the frontier environment. He virtually ignored the role of women, blacks, Indians, Mormons, Hispanics and Asians in shaping the diverse human geography of the Western United States. Though the West was widely regarded as the home of individualism, members of frontier communities usually found that they had to act collectively. Joint effort was needed to deal with problems of law enforcement, to secure protection against Indian attack, and even to carry out normal pioneering tasks.

It is easier to argue that white settlers had more impact on the Western frontier than the Western frontier had on white settlers. In little more than a generation, a tide of white settlement had swept over the area. The power of the Indian tribes was broken and their hunting grounds became the domain of miners, cattlemen and farmers. The growing demand for orderly government in the West led to the hasty creation of territories: Dakota, Colorado and Nevada territories were created in 1861: the Idaho and Arizona territories in 1863 and the Montana territory in 1864. Silver-rich Nevada gained statehood in 1864. The admission of a host of new states was delayed because of party divisions in Congress where Democrats were reluctant to create states that were likely to be solidly Republican. After the admission of Colorado in 1876, no new states were admitted until the end of the 1880s. Unfortunately, many of the territorial officials, appointed by the federal government, were third-rate hacks who were usually appointed because of who they knew rather than what they knew. Very few served for more than four years. The weakness of the territorial government encouraged Westerners to take the law into their own hands.

The frontier experience of those men and women who settled in the Wild West caught the imagination of contemporary Easterners. As farmers, miners, ranchers and prostitutes pursued their various activities in the real West, a parallel legendary West took deep roots in the American imagination. In the nineteenth century this mythic West was shaped primarily by Western dime novels which Erastus Beadle began publishing in 1860. These novels, and the many imitators, featuring such legendary (albeit real-life) characters as Buffalo Bill and Calamity Jane, sold in huge numbers. The novels familiarised readers with a world of stagecoaches and outlaws, gold rushes, buffalo herds and Indians. Stories of some of the Western heroes became powerful forces for morality and social order. Romantic pictorial representations of the West were also influential in shaping popular conception. The two most highly regarded Western artists, Charles Russell and Frederic Remington, drew on first hand experience. Although their romantic images did not always correspond with reality, by emphasising the qualities Americans admired most - manliness, individualism, self-reliance - they made the West an acceptable image of American society as a whole. The Wild West continued to fascinate future generations when adapted to cinema and television in the twentieth century. Both media also tended to romanticise Western life.

The settlement of the West had its romantic and heroic side. It can certainly be seen as a great achievement - a formidable episode in the social, economic and political history of the USA. But the cost of that achievement in human and natural terms was considerable. The brutality of the Indian wars and the destruction of the Indian culture was a significant part of the human cost. But by no means all white settlers prospered. The mining, cattle and cereal bonanzas set in motion boom or bust economics in which a few became fabulously wealthy: many others, in contrast, barely survived. In natural terms, the Western pioneers left behind a trail of waste and devastation, wantonly slaughtering wild life, squandering the West's mineral wealth, ruining the soil by unwise farming methods, and felling huge forests. By the 1870s some Americans were concerned at both the threat to the forests and the destruction of the West's natural beauty. Little was done on the timber conservation front until the early twentieth century. However, the first National Park in the USA - indeed in the world - was created in March 1872 when Congress passed an act designating two million acres of Wyoming Territory as Yellowstone National Park. This area of natural wonders, with its geysers, waterfalls and mountains, was set apart as a public park for the enjoyment of the people. But powerful economic influences remained hostile to the National Park concept and not until the late nineteenth century was the Yellowstone formula extended.

Making notes on 'The Winning of the West'

You may need to make fairly full notes on this chapter if only because examiners can ask a great variety of questions on the development of the West. Your notes should help you understand the process by which the West was won and also some of the consequences of that process. You may well need to know a reasonable amount about United States' Indian policy. Why were the Indians beaten? Did they ever stand a chance? With the benefit of hindsight, what should have been United States policy with regard to the Indians? One of the major concerns of this book is to determine the results of the Civil War. I contend that the Civil War had relatively little impact on Western development which continued through the war years. Actions of the Republican-controlled Congress during the War may have speeded up the winning of the West. But I am convinced that Western expansion, long a feature of American history, would have happened anyway. I think I would also be happier arguing that the results of late nineteenth-century Western expansion had a greater impact on American development than the results of Civil War and Reconstruction. Would you?

Answering essay questions on 'The Winning of the West'

It is likely you will use evidence from this chapter to answer specific questions about the American West. Consider the following:

1 Why was the American West opened up so quickly after 1865?
2 Was there anything 'heroic' or 'romantic' in the winning of the West after 1865?
3 Account for the destruction of the Plains Indians' way of life in the late nineteenth century.

In all history essays the first paragraph is often crucial. It is the first opportunity for you to impress (or depress) an examiner and convince him/her that you understand the question. There is no perfect way of writing an introduction but there are certain things you ought to be trying to do. Firstly you should be trying to establish the precise meaning of the question. This often involves defining the most important terms in the title and also identifying the periods of time which are relevant. You should also be identifying the key issues within the question which you will go on to develop. Finally you should also outline your basic argument. It is a waste of precious time and space to say (as many students do) that you are going to answer the question. Hopefully you are so get on and do it from the start!

Try to write an introduction for question 1. Attempt to compose a good opening sentence. Go on to identify the periods of time which are relevant. You might say that much of the West was opened up by 1880. The declaration of the superintendent of the census in 1890 is often taken as the symbolic end of the Western frontier. Nevertheless, there were still some remote Western areas where there was sparse white settlement in the early years of the twentieth century. What factors led to the opening up of the West? Which factor(s) do you see as being most significant?

Another essential part of any essay is the final paragraph or conclusion. In this you should be recapping, drawing together the threads of your argument and finally giving your opinion on the central issue in the question set. Your conclusion should not be loaded down with factual information. Nor should you spring some new and previously unexplored idea that you have just thought of on the reader. The conclusion should stem logically from the rest of the essay. Do not be afraid to give your view: after all, this is what questions usually ask for.

Try writing a conclusion of six to eight sentences for question 2. What was 'romantic' and 'heroic' about the opening up of the West? What was not 'romantic' and not 'heroic'? Try to reach a balanced conclusion but note that this does not mean you should sit on the fence. Now write both an introduction and a conclusion, both of some six to eight sentences, for question 3.

Source-based questions on 'The Winning of the West'

1 Western settlement
Examine the poster on page 121. Answer the following questions:
a)   How does the poster attempt to attract settlers to the West? (5 marks)
b)   What does the poster not say about life in the West? (5 marks)
c)   The poster exaggerates the attractiveness of the West. Does this mean that it has little value as a source? (5 marks)
d)   Posters apart, how else might potential settlers have obtained information about Western lands? (5 marks)

2 Artists' impressions of the West
Examine the illustrations on pages 136 and 137. Answer the following questions:
a)   What does the illustration on page 136 suggest about the strengths and weaknesses of the US army in the Indian wars? (5 marks)
b)   How might it be possible to check the extent to which this source is reliable? (5 marks)

c) Which of the two illustrations on pages 136 and 137 do you think is the best source for helping us understand what happened at the battle of the Little Bighorn? Explain your answer. (10 marks)

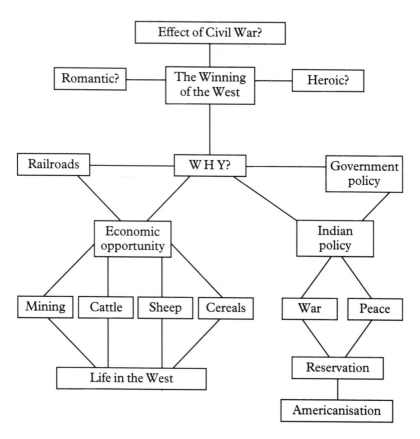

Summary - The Winning of the West

CHAPTER 7

Conclusion: The Second American Revolution?

1 America's Second Revolution?

Abraham Lincoln had not set out in 1861 with the intention of waging a revolutionary struggle. Indeed, in his first message to Congress in December 1861 he deplored that prospect. However, in March 1865 Lincoln talked of the 'fundamental and astounding' changes which had occurred as a result of the war. Many contemporaries saw things similarly. In 1869 an American historian George Ticknor declared that the Civil War had riven 'a great gulf between what happened before in our century and what has happened since or what is likely to happen hereafter. It does not seem to me as if I were living in the country in which I was born'.

If Northerners (like Ticknor) viewed the Civil War and its aftermath as revolutionary, white Southerners had even more cause to do so. Defeat and slave emancipation seemed to have resulted in massive political, social and economic changes in the South. An anguished Memphis newspaper editor declared in 1865 that 'the events of the last five years have produced an entire revolution in the entire Southern country'. Many late nineteenth-century Europeans also saw the Civil War as a revolution. The French politician Georges Clemenceau spoke of it as 'one of the most radical revolutions known to history'. Karl Marx, who was writing *Das Kapital* - a vast treatise on revolution - while the war was taking place, had no doubts that it amounted to a revolution (even though it did not fit happily into his all-embracing theory of class revolution).

Twentieth-century historians have held differing opinions on the impact of the war. Some, like Beard, Degler and McPherson have been convinced that the Civil War was indeed America's second revolution. But others have remained sceptical. The debate is complicated by the fact that historians sometimes examine the Civil War and reconstruction as two distinct topics. It is thus possible to view the effects of the Civil War as revolutionary - and reconstruction as at best a half-finished - and at worst a failed - revolution. It is also possible to regard reconstruction, and not the war, as the real revolution!

Another problem is the word 'revolution' which means different things to different people at different times. The word implies massive - and usually sudden - political, social and/or economic change. Few would argue that the Civil War did not affect most Americans' lives. It became a total war and, like many total wars, snowballed into huge and unanticipated dimensions, taking on a life and purpose of its own far beyond the causes that had started it. However, the First and Second

World Wars did just the same - possibly more so. These twentieth century total wars are not normally regarded as revolutions, even though they brought about great changes both to Europe and the world.

2 The Emancipation of the Slaves

The main evidence in support of the war being revolutionary is that it resulted in the emancipation of some 4,000,000 slaves. It is difficult to see how this would have occurred without the Civil War. Some have argued that slavery would have withered and died in the last decades of the nineteenth century. But this can never be more than conjecture. The reality was that Southerners were so determined to preserve their peculiar institution that they waged war for four terrible years. Southern slaveholders had billions of dollars (trillions by today's reckoning) invested in slavery. Even the 75 per cent of white Southerners who had no direct economic stake in slavery believed it to be an essential form of social control. Given this situation, it seems unlikely that Southerners would have quickly or easily accepted the end of slavery. Nor had Lincoln, even though he abhorred it, any intentions of threatening slavery where it already existed in 1861.

In 1865 the federal government, as a result of winning the war, was able to confiscate the principal form of property in one third of the country. This confiscation, without compensation, was without parallel in American history. It had a major impact on both slaveholder and slave. Although the ex-slaves did not achieve as much as they had hoped, black per capita income did increase after 1865. By 1880 20 per cent of black farm operatives owned part or all of the land that they farmed. By 1900 about 50 per cent of American blacks were literate. Moreover, if only for a relatively short period, the ex-slaves were elevated to civil and political equality with whites.

Some historians, while accepting that the emancipation of the slaves was certainly one of the major accomplishments of the Civil War, have questioned whether it amounted to a revolution. While emancipation affected some 4,000,000 ex-slaves and some 350,000 slaveholders, it had little impact on the majority of - Northern - Americans. Arguably no great social or race relations revolution occurred in the South. In the ex-Confederate states blacks remained second-class citizens. Dominance of the Southern economy by the old planter class continued after 1865. By devices such as share cropping, planters kept their black labour force subservient and poor. By the start of the twentieth century blacks had lost most of their civil and political rights. White attitudes to blacks had not changed: indeed they may have hardened. Whatever paternalistic feelings had existed pre-1861, they were no longer much in evidence after 1865.

3 Nationalism

It is possible to argue that the main result of the Civil War was that it ensured that the Union survived as a single, indissoluble nation. Some think the 'fiery trial' actually created, and defined, the modern United States. Certainly the war settled the question of state rights. No American since 1865 has doubted where sovereignty ultimately lies. However, it is difficult to argue that the restoration of the status quo was a revolutionary event. It is also hard to claim that the war created an American nation or a sense of American nationalism. Perhaps soldiers and civilians alike, as a result of their blood, sweat, toil and tears, developed a sense of belonging to a nation: perhaps the war also gave America a new set of heroes and memories which a sense of nationality demands. But American nationalism - both in the North and in the South - had been remarkably strong in the early nineteenth century. Indeed, one of the main causes of Union success in the Civil War was the fact that most Northerners were intensely nationalistic: hundreds of thousands of men were prepared to fight and die for their country. Although Southerners returned to the fold after 1865, many continued to think of themselves first and foremost as Southerners. It should also be said that the Union that survived the Civil War was far from a centralised, unified state: it remained a Union of individual states.

4 The Balance of Government

Some historians claim that after 1865 the federal government had a far greater involvement in most Americans' lives than it had before the war. Certainly, during the course of the war two things occurred: federal government's powers and responsibilities increased enormously; and Lincoln massively extended presidential power. The old decentralised federal republic became a new national polity that conscripted young men into the armed forces, taxed people directly (and heavily), expanded the jurisdiction of the federal courts and interfered in many aspects of economic life. After 1865 federal expenditure and taxation remained well above pre-war levels. The national banking system survived. Even the greenbacks continued a somewhat precarious existence. The wartime legislation on railroads, public lands and tariffs was consolidated - not abandoned - post 1865. The changes wrought by the war, it is often implied, were not undone, largely because the war years resulted in a major change in ideology. This claim can (apparently) be substantiated by examination of changes to the constitution. The first ten constitutional amendments had set out to limit national authority. But after the Civil War, six of the next seven amendments empowered the federal government to act. Congress, for example, now had the power to end slavery, protect civil rights and end racial discrimination in voting. After 1865 federal power was seen as the guarantor, not the nemesis, of liberty.

However, it is possible to argue that the war years were an aberration. It was inevitable that during the conflict federal power would increase. (Some think it is surprising how limited that increase was.) After the war, there was a return to 'normalcy'. The rapid demobilisation of the army in 1865 is a good example of the hasty abandonment of the government's wartime powers. Washington scaled down its efforts to manage the nation's financial system: many of the wartime sources of revenue (like income tax) ended; and the government slashed its own expenditure. For the rest of the nineteenth century, the Washington government had a minimal impact on the lives of most Americans. Belief in state rights and the notion of a weak federal government remained articles of faith of most Americans - and not just Southerners. The 14th and 15th Amendments may (in theory) have reduced the power of the individual states. But in practice they did not expand the power of the federal government which lacked the effective power - and will - to enforce and execute the general principles contained within the Amendments. While Lincoln had undoubtedly extended presidential power during the war, he had been entitled to do so because of his constitutional powers as Commander-in-Chief. But after 1865 executive authority rapidly contracted - as Andrew Johnson found to his cost. For the rest of the nineteenth century, no President came near to wielding Lincoln's power. Now that the Union was safe, the Supreme Court felt free to resume its role of watchdog on the excesses of all aspects of government.

5 The Economic and Social Effects

It is certainly possible to claim that the war had massive economic effects on both North and South. The historian Charles Beard saw the war as the triumph of the forces of industrialism and free labour capitalism over slave labour plantation agriculture. The war, in Beard's view, was 'a social cataclysm ... making vast changes in the arrangement of classes, in the distribution of wealth, in the course of industrial development'. Marxist historians have also portrayed the war as a great capitalist, bourgeois triumph. While most historians today regard such views as far too sweeping, some would argue that the Civil War did nourish the growth of Northern business enterprise, ensuring that the USA became the world's greatest economic force after 1865. During the war, the Republican Party was able to pass a broad spectrum of economic laws (previously blocked by the Southern-dominated Democrat Party) which underpinned the country's future economic growth: higher tariffs; a national banking system; land grants and government loans to build the first transcontinental railroad; and the Homestead Act granting 160 acres of government land to Western settlers. Arguably these measures did more to reshape the relations of the federal government to the economy than any previous or future legislation (except for the first hundred days of the New Deal in 1933). The measures might well have helped open up the West, an area vital to the USA's industrial growth. Republican policies (as well as the demands of the war itself) may also have encouraged the growth of big business. Certainly many of the great financiers and industrialists of the late nineteenth century were set on the path to wealth and power by the Civil War. Men like Carnegie and Rockefeller benefited from the great business opportunities that it offered. Nor did they forget the lessons it taught, especially the advantage of large-scale enterprise. It may be, that, henceforward, the most successful American businessmen thought not in local but in national - even international - terms. It has also been claimed that Northern agriculture underwent revolutionary change during the war years, the shortage of labour forcing farmers to invest in agricultural machinery.

However, there are many counter arguments to the notion that the war resulted in major economic change. The USA, after all, had been a great economic power, second only to Britain, before 1861. The crucial innovations in transport, agriculture and manufacturing had begun well before 1861. The war may have accelerated some of these developments, but it produced no fundamental change of direction. While Northern industrial might ensured Northern triumph, it is possible that the war actually retarded the country's industrial growth rate. The 1860s show up poorly in statistical terms when measured against earlier and later decades.

The extent to which the war affected the Southern economy is also a subject of some debate. The South was essentially an agrarian society before the war. It remained essentially agrarian thereafter. During the war - fought mainly on Southern soil - Northern soldiers inflicted considerable damage and destruction on all aspects of the Southern economy - railroads, farms and livestock. But, on the positive side, agricultural resources were not easily destroyed by nineteenth century warfare. It was relatively easy to replace lost material with relatively little capital. Arguably this is what happened. Most Southern railroads, for example, were restored to operating order by 1870 and thereafter the number of railroads greatly increased. By 1877, the South seemed to have recovered from the destruction and dislocation caused by the war. In 1877 the output of all the South's distinctive crops - with the exception of sugar - was similar to that in 1860. The cotton crop of 1875 broke the 1859 record of 4,500,000 bales and by 1878 production exceeded 5,000,000 bales. By 1878-9 the South had regained its share of the world cotton market (thanks partly to the collapse of supplies from India). Although the South remained essentially agrarian, there was considerable industrial and urban development after 1865. By 1869 total manufacturing output greatly exceeded that of 1860. White wage-earners may have gained something from the removal of competition from cheap slave labour.

But the Southern economy did face problems. In the two decades before the war per capita income in the South had increased at a faster rate than in the North. By 1860 the average per capita income level enjoyed by the South's free men and women was marginally above the levels enjoyed by Northerners. But Southern incomes fell by nearly 40 per cent in the years from 1860 to 1870. By 1880 per capita income levels had reached a standard little better than 40 years earlier. Agriculture continued to dominate the economic life of the South. Most land and productive capital remained under the control of a minority of white owners. But after 1865 agricultural production fell significantly. This was largely because freedmen and women refused to work like slaves. The sharecropping systems and credit arrangements which evolved out of bargaining between poor black and white farmers and property owners after 1865 have been condemned for restraining growth and diversification in the Southern economy. Small farms were probably not as efficient as plantations which benefited from economies of scale and from the fact that they could force slaves to work long hours. Some economic historians claim that Southern farmers paid excessively high payment of interest to merchants/storekeepers - or rents to landowners. The merchants and landowners have been charged with promoting an overproduction of cash crops - especially cotton - which at first sight seemed more profitable than the cultivation of food crops. Storekeepers, looking after their own interests, refused credit on lien of crops other than cotton. Year after year poor sharecroppers (especially blacks), in need of credit and desperate for cash to pay off increasing debts, were forced to grow more cotton. Thus poor farmers had less than sovereign control over the choice of their crops and devoted a higher percentage of the tilled acreage to cotton than did larger farmers. The result was that after 1865 the South became a net importer of food and poor farmers were steadily less self-sufficient in food production. Age-old labour-intensive methods of cultivating the soil and harvesting the cotton crop remained the norm. There was thus low productivity of labour. Urbanisation and industrial development did not proceed rapidly enough to push real wages and per capita incomes up to Northern levels. The South remained the poorest section of the USA and black Southerners remained the poorest group within the South.

The social effects of the war, the emancipation of slaves apart, were limited. Certainly in the North, the war produced no massive upheaval in the social order. Those who claim that the war fostered the conditions which resulted in rapid urbanisation and industrialisation, have argued that the war helped clear the way for a system in which the typical worker was the wage-earning employee of a huge corporation, with little or no prospect of ever achieving the traditional kind of economic independence as a reward for his/her labours. But this state of affairs would almost certainly have occurred with or without the war. Most Americans

- indeed most members of trade unions which made some gains during the war - shared the prevailing 'free labour' ideology. There was little sense of working-class solidarity and few wanted social revolution. There was no social revolution as far as women were concerned. If the Civil War had opened up doors of opportunity for women, those doors were quickly closed both North and South. Nor did the loss of 620,000 young men have a major social - or economic - effect. Natural increase and high immigration ensured that by 1870 the American population far exceeded that of 1860.

6 International Implications

The war had few major international repercussions. It remained purely an American conflict. For a while the USA was the world's greatest military and naval power. But after 1865 the country quickly demobilised its armed forces. During the war, European powers did not involve themselves in America's internal struggle. For five decades thereafter, the USA did not involve itself in European affairs. Only in the Western hemisphere were the international repercussions of the war immediately obvious. After 1865 the primacy of the USA in the Western hemisphere was established beyond all doubt. The French retreat from Mexico (1867) and Russia's sale of Alaska (1867) to the USA symbolised the USA's power on the North American continent. Even (perhaps especially!) Britain conceded hegemony to the USA in the Americas. The settlement of the West led the United States government to a greater economic and strategic interest in the Pacific region. Rich in people and resources, the USA was a potential major world power by 1877. But this would almost certainly have happened with or without the Civil War.

7 The Political Effects

The war had some major political effects. It brought a few new men to the fore. War heroes, like Grant, now played important political roles. Some of these men, although probably not Grant himself, might well have become politicians anyway. But the main political result of the war was the effect it had on the sectional balance of power. Between 1789 and 1861, a Southern slaveholder had been President of the country for 49 years; 23 of the 36 speakers of the House had been Southerners; and the Supreme Court had always had a Southern majority. After the war a hundred years passed before a resident of an ex-Confederate state was elected President. For 50 years none of the speakers of the House came from the South. Only 5 of the 26 Supreme Court justices appointed during the next 50 years were Southerners. McPherson is convinced that this transformation in the balance of political power between North and South merits the label of revolution. But arguably this Northern dominance would have happened anyway. Indeed, the fact that it seemed about to happen (as far as Southerners were concerned) had actually led to Civil War in 1861.

The Civil War also appears to be a watershed in the history of American political parties. The Democrat Party had been the dominant force in the three decades before 1860. In the 70 years after 1860 only two Democrat Presidents occupied the White House. The Republican Party, living for decades on its reputation as the party of Abraham Lincoln and the party which saved the Union and freed the slaves, dominated American politics. However, once the Southern states returned to full participation in national politics in the 1870s, the Republican position was anything but secure. The five presidential elections from 1876 to 1892 were extremely close-run affairs. Two were won by the Democrat Grover Cleveland. Only one of the three Republican victors, James Garfield, had a clear majority in the total vote. In the ten Congressional elections between 1874 and 1892 the Democrats won a clear - and sometimes a large - majority of seats in the House of Representatives on eight occasions. Republican efforts to win support in the South - which fluctuated between bids to attract and organise the black vote and attempts to create a white Republican Party in the South - produced no significant success. Not until 1896 did the Republican Party win a presidential election by a considerable majority - for reasons which had relatively little to do with the Civil War.

8 Conclusion

Mark Twain wrote that the Civil War had 'uprooted institutions that were centuries old ... transformed the social life of half the country, and wrought so profoundly upon the entire national character'. Twain may have exaggerated the effect of the war on the American character. But he was surely correct to stress that the war had a massive impact on 'half' the country. While it is easier to see continuity than revolution in the North, the Civil War undoubtedly had a dramatic impact on the South - an impact that might fairly be described as 'revolutionary'. The war overthrew the South's social and political system: by 1865 the plantation system and slavery were gone; and the South had lost much of its national economic and political power.

From a white Southern perspective, things might have been worse. Although humbled by defeat, white Southerners soon found a new pride in the memory of the 'lost cause'. Emancipation did not result in racial warfare, social anarchy and total economic collapse as pro-slavers had predicted before 1861. Southern whites salvaged what they could from the wreck of defeat and their 'counter-revolution' had some success. By 1877 all the Southern states had white conservative or Democrat-controlled governments. Notwithstanding the 14th and 15th Amendments, white supremacy was restored. The majority of American blacks had no equal civil rights until the second half of the twentieth century. But relatively few of the 2,000,000 Northerners who fought in the Civil War had been fighting for black civil rights. The end of slavery and the passing of the 14th and 15th Amendments were extraordinary developments in terms of what might have been anticipated in 1861. In that sense, the changes wrought by the war were indeed revolutionary.

Working on *'Conclusion: The Second American Revolution?'*

This chapter assesses the results of the Civil War and reconstruction period, particularly the extent to which the events described in the rest of the book can be considered to be revolutionary. Major changes usually occur as a result of major wars. But most major European wars are not regarded as revolutions. Many historians think that revolution is an over-used word. Is it an appropriate word to describe developments in the USA in the 1860s and 1870s?

It is worthwhile thinking about the following essay title:

> To what extent should the American Civil War and Reconstruction be considered 'America's second revolution'?

You should by now have realised the importance of composing first paragraphs for essays and should be able to do so quite quickly. Unfortunately you still have seven or eight other paragraphs to write! Make a detailed plan to indicate the main themes of these paragraphs. Finally you must bring the essay to a rational conclusion. Were the changes brought about by the Civil War and its aftermath of such proportion that the word 'revolution' is appropriate?

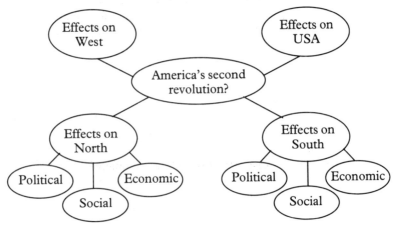

Summary - Conclusion: The Second American Revolution?

Chronological Table

1861	April	Start of the Civil War
1862	May	Homestead Act
	Sept	Sioux War broke out in Minnesota
1863	Dec	President Lincoln issued Proclamation of Amnesty and Reconstruction
1864	Aug	Wade-Davis bill vetoed by Lincoln
	Oct	Nevada admitted to the Union
	Nov	Massacre of Cheyennes at Sand Creek, Colorado
1865	March	Freedmen's Bureau established.
	April	Lincoln assassinated: Andrew Johnson became President
	May	End of fighting in the Civil War
	May	Johnson issued Proclamation of Amnesty and Reconstruction
	May-Dec	Ex-Confederate states held constitutional conventions
	Dec	Thirteenth Amendment added to the Constitution
	Dec	Presidential Reconstruction completed
	Dec	Start of Ku Klux Klan in Tennessee
1866	April	Congress enacted the Civil Rights Act
	May	Race riots in Memphis
	July	Race riots in New Orleans
	Nov	Republicans won mid-term Congressional elections
	Dec	Fetterman massacre
1867	March	First Republican Reconstruction Act
	March	Nebraska admitted to the Union
	April	USA purchased Alaska from Russia
	Sept	First shipment of longhorn cattle from Abilene
	Nov	House Joint Committee voted to impeach President Johnson
	Nov	Medicine Lodge Treaty
1868	April	Fort Laramie Treaty
	May	President Johnson was acquitted on impeachment charges
	July	Fourteenth Amendment added to the Constitution
	Nov	Ulysses S. Grant elected President
1869	March	Public Credit Act
	May	Transcontinental railroad completed
	Sept	Failure of Gould and Fish's scheme to corner gold market
	Dec	Formation of Knights of Labor

1870	Jan	John D. Rockefeller formed Standard Oil Company
	Feb	First African American took seat in Senate
	March	Fifteenth Amendment added to the Constitution
	June	Senate rejected plan to annex Santo Domingo
	Dec	All ex-Confederate states restored to Union
1871	March	Civil Service commission established
	April	Ku Klux Klan Act
	July	Exposure of Tweed Ring
1872	May	Liberal Republican Party formed
	June	End of Freedmen Bureau
	Sept	Credit Mobilier scandal
	Sept	'Alabama' claim settled
	Nov	Grant re-elected President
1873	Sept	Start of 'Panic of 1873'
1874	Aug	Custer announced gold discovered in Black Hills of South Dakota
	Nov	Democrats gained control of the House of Representatives
1875	Jan	Specie Resumption Act
	March	Civil Rights Act
	May	Whisky scandal exposed
	Sept	Conviction of Molly Maguires
1876	March	First transmission of sound over wire
	May/June	Philadelphia World Fair
	June	Battle of the Little Bighorn
	August	Colorado admitted to the Union
	Nov	Disputed Presidential election
1877	March	Rutherford B. Hayes inaugurated President
	July	First national rail strike
	Oct	Surrender of Nez Perce Chief Joseph
1890	Dec	Massacre at Wounded Knee

Further Reading

You will not be surprised to learn that there are hundreds of excellent books on Reconstruction, the Wild West, the process of industrialisation, political developments in the Gilded Age, and the results of the American Civil War. It is impossible for most students to consult more than just a few of these. However, it is vital that you read some, particularly if you are taking the period as a special or depth study. The period from 1865 to 1877 is one of considerable controversy and you will be in a better position to form your own conclusions if you have read widely. The following suggestions are meant to serve as a guide from which you might wish to 'pick and mix'.

1. General Works

There are surprisingly few books which deal with this period as a whole. **Eric Foner's** *Reconstruction: America's Unfinished Revolution 1863-1877* (Harper and Row, 1988) concentrates mainly on developments in the South but does examine the situation elsewhere, and remains probably the best general work. **James M. McPherson,** *Ordeal by Fire: The Civil War and Reconstruction* (McGraw, 1982) has some useful chapters. **James G. Randall and David H. Donald,** *The Civil War and Reconstruction* (D.C. Heath and Company, 1969) provides an overview.

2 Reconstruction and the South

Eric Foner's *Reconstruction* (op cit) is the best text, providing a thorough exploration of reconstruction and stressing the centrality of the black experience. Other useful surveys include **Kenneth M. Stampp,** *The Era of Reconstruction, 1865-1877* (Knopf, 1965) and **John Hope Franklin,** *Reconstruction after the Civil War* (University of Chicago Press, 1961). **Eric Anderson and Alfred A. Moss** (eds), *The Facts of Reconstruction: Essays in Honour of John Hope Franklin* (Louisiana State University Press, 1991) is a splendid collection of essays. Also try **Michael Perman,** *Reunion without Compromise: The South and Reconstruction 1865-1868* (University of North Carolina Press, 1973) and *The Road to Redemption: Southern Politics, 1869-1879* (University of North Carolina Press, 1984). On economic, social and political matters post-reconstruction read **Gavin Wright,** *Old South, New South: Revolutions in the Southern Economy Since the Civil War* (Basic, 1986), **C Vann Woodward's** classic work, *Origins of the New South, 1877-1913* (Oxford University Press, 1951), **C. Vann Woodward's** *The Strange Career of Jim Crow* (Oxford University Press 3rd edition, 1974) and **Joel Williamson,** *The Crucible of Race: Black-White Relations in the American*

South Since Emancipation (Oxford University Press, 1984). **Hans Trefousse,** *Andrew Johnson: A Biography* (Norton and Company, 1989) is perhaps the best work on Johnson although **Eric McKitrick,** *Andrew Johnson and Reconstruction* (University of Chicago Press, 1960) is still worth reading.

3 Northern Economy and Society

The best brief introductions are **Glenn Porter,** *The Rise of Big Business,* (Harlan Davidson, rev. edition 1992), **Thomas C. Cochran and William Miller,** *The Age of Enterprise: A Social History of Industrial America* (Macmillan, 1951), **Robert L. Heilbroner and Aaron Singer,** *The Economic Transformation of America* (HarperCollins, rev edition 1984), and **Stuart Bruckey,** *Enterprise: The Dynamic Economy of a Free People* (Harvard University Press, 1990). The inventions that made possible the economic revolution are described in **Nathan Rosenberg,** *Technology and American Economic Growth* (M.E. Sharpe, 1972). Technological advances in manufacturing are covered in **D.G. Houndsell,** *From the American System to Mass Production* (John Hopkins University Press, 1984). Railroads' contribution to economic growth are best studied in **Albro Martin's** *Railroads Triumphant* (Oxford University Press, 1991). **Charles A. Glaab and A. Theodore Brown,** *A History of Urban America* (Macmillan, 3rd edition, 1983) is a good starting point for urban development.. Try also **Gunther P. Barth,** *City People: The Rise of Modern City Culture in Nineteenth Century America* (Oxford University Press, 1980). **David Montgomery,** *The Fall of the House of Labor: The Workplace, the State, and American Labor Activism 1865-1925* (Cambridge University Press, 1987) analyses the transformation of industrial production and its impact on labour. **Olivier Zunz,** *Making America Corporate, 1870-1920* (University of Chicago Press, 1990) examines corporate capitalism's impact on the creation of a consumer culture. **Alan Trachtenberg,** *The Incorporation of America: Culture and Society in the Gilded Age* (Hill and Wang, 1982) is also useful. The most concise and readable study of Carnegie is **Harold C. Livesay,** *Andrew Carnegie and the Rise of Big Business* (Little Brown, 1975). **Allan Nevins,** *Study in Power: John D. Rockefeller, industrialist and philanthropist* 2 vols (Scribner's, 1953) remains a classic but **David F. Hawke,** *John D.: The Founding Father of the Rockefellers* (Harper, 1980) is more balanced. For women's role see **Catherine Clinton,** *The Other Civil War: American Women in the Nineteenth Century* (Hill and Wang, 1984).

4 Northern Politics

A relatively recent synthesis is **Sean Dennis Cashman,** *America in the*

Gilded Age: From the Death of Lincoln to the Rise of Theodore Roosevelt (New York University Press, 1984). **William Gillette,** *Retreat from Reconstruction, 1869-1879* (Louisiana State University Press, 1979) also provides a survey of the national politics of the period. Historians have had difficulty making Grant an interesting figure but **William S. McFeely's** *Grant* (Norton and Company, 1980) is the most up-to-date and authoritative study. **Earle Dudley Ross,** *The Liberal Republican Movement* (University of Washington, 1969) is still worth consulting. **Roberty L. Beisner,** *From the Old Diplomacy to the New 1865-1900* (Harlan Davidson, 2nd edition 1986) deals with US foreign policy in the period as does **Walter LaFeber,** *New Empire: American Expansionism 1860-1898* (Cornell University Press, 1963).

5 The West

The most useful general surveys of the trans-Mississippi West are **Ray Allen Billington and Martin Ridge,** *Westward Expansion* (Macmillan, 5th edition 1982) and **C.A. Milne, C.O. Connor and M.A. Sandweiss,** *The Oxford History of the American West* (Oxford University Press, 1994). On the Indian wars, see **Robert M. Utley,** *The Indian Frontier of the American West, 1846-1890* (University of New Mexico Press, 1984). A strongly pro-Indian but very unreliable popular account is **Dee Brown,** *Bury My Heart at Wounded Knee* (Vintage, 1970). **William T. Hagan,** *American Indians* (University of Chicago, 1964) and **Robert M. Utley,** *Cavalier in Buckskin: George Armstrong Custer and the Western Military Frontier* (University of Oklahoma Press, 1988) are much better reads. **Gilbert G. Fite,** *The Farmers' Frontier, 1865-1900* (University of Oklahoma Press, 1966) is a solid introduction to farming on the Great Plains. On cowboys try **William R. Savage,** *The Cowboy Hero: His Image in American History and Culture* (University of Oklahoma Press, 1986)

Index

This book is to be returned on or before the last date below.

-7. APR. 1997

-8. MAY 1997

-8 NOV 2002

28 NOV 2002

26 NOV 2004

10 DEC 2004

2 9 OCT 2007

1 4 JUL 2008

2 - NOV 2009

-6 JUN 2011